Kentucky Bourbon: The Pride of the Bluegrass State
Di Tran Bourbon BELIEF: Bridging American Bourbon to the World

Kentucky Bourbon: The Pride of the Bluegrass State
Di Tran Bourbon BELIEF: Bridging American Bourbon to the World

Copyright © 2024 by Di Tran Enterprise

All rights reserved.

No part of this book may be reproduced, stored in a retrieval system, or transmitted in any form or by any means—electronic, mechanical, photocopying, recording, or otherwise—without the prior written permission of the publisher, except for the use of brief quotations in a book review or scholarly journal.

The content provided in this book is intended solely for educational and motivational purposes. It is not intended to serve as a substitute for professional advice. Should you require professional advice, please consult a qualified professional.

The publisher and the author make no representations or warranties with respect to the accuracy, applicability, fitness, or completeness of the contents of this book. They disclaim any warranties (expressed or implied), merchantability, or fitness for any particular purpose. The publisher and the author shall in no event be held liable for any loss or other damages, including but not limited to special, incidental, consequential, or other damages. The views

Kentucky Bourbon: The Pride of the Bluegrass State
Di Tran Bourbon BELIEF: Bridging American Bourbon to the World

expressed are those of the author alone and should not be taken as expert advice.

The information in this book is provided "as is," and when you use this information, you do so at your own risk. The contents of this book are intended to provide helpful and accurate information regarding the topics discussed. The publisher and author are not liable for the use or misuse of any materials or information contained in this book.

While every attempt has been made to verify the information provided in this publication, neither the author nor the publisher assumes any responsibility for errors, omissions, or contradictory information contained in this book. Any perceived slights of specific persons, peoples, or organizations are unintentional.

Kentucky Bourbon: The Pride of the Bluegrass State
Di Tran Bourbon BELIEF: Bridging American Bourbon to the World

Contents

Copyright © 2024 by Di Tran Enterprise 2

Introduction: "Vietnamese Born and American Made" 6

Chapter 1: The Heart of Kentucky – A Legacy of Bourbon 12

Chapter 2: Kentucky Bourbon – A Class of Its Own . 22

Chapter 3: BELIEF – More Than a Drink 33

Chapter 4: The Cultural Tapestry of Kentucky 43

Chapter 5: Bourbon vs. The World 54

Chapter 6: The Craft of Belief – Creating Di Tran Bourbon 65

Chapter 7: A Toast to Humanity 75

Chapter 8: Beyond the Bottle – The Legacy of Di Tran Bourbon 85

Chapter 9: The Global Spirit of Kentucky 96

Chapter 10: The Future of Bourbon – Continuing the Tradition 105

THE END 122

THANK YOU 122

Kentucky Bourbon: The Pride of the Bluegrass State
Di Tran Bourbon BELIEF: Bridging American Bourbon to the World

Introduction: "Vietnamese Born and American Made"

A Journey Begins

The story of Di Tran begins not in the rolling hills of Kentucky, where bourbon flows as freely as the stories passed down through generations, but in the bustling streets of Vietnam. Born into a culture rich with tradition and history, Di Tran's early years were shaped by the values of his homeland—family, hard work, and resilience. Yet, like many immigrants, his story is one of transformation, of finding a new home in a place far from where his journey began.

Di Tran arrived in the United States as a young man, full of dreams and aspirations, but also burdened with the challenges that come with leaving everything familiar behind. Kentucky, a state known for its hospitality and warmth, became the place where Di Tran would not only find his footing but also discover a new passion—bourbon. It was here that the story of "Vietnamese Born and American Made" truly began to unfold, as Kentucky opened its arms to Di Tran, offering him not just a place to live, but a community that embraced him as one of its own.

The Cultural Shift: From Cognac to Bourbon

Kentucky Bourbon: The Pride of the Bluegrass State
Di Tran Bourbon BELIEF: Bridging American Bourbon to the World

Growing up in Vietnam, Di Tran was accustomed to the traditions of his culture, including the preference for certain spirits. In many Asian households, brandy, particularly Cognac XO, was the drink of choice. It was a symbol of sophistication and status, a drink reserved for special occasions and gatherings with family and friends. Di Tran, like many of his peers, grew up associating this rich, amber liquid with moments of celebration and connection.

However, upon his arrival in Kentucky, Di Tran was introduced to a different kind of spirit—bourbon. At first, the idea of bourbon was foreign to him. It was strong, unrefined in its approach, and so very American. But as he settled into his new life, Di Tran began to explore the local culture, and with it, the world of bourbon. It was during this time that he was introduced to Buffalo Trace George T. Stagg, a bourbon that would change his perception of what a drink could be.

The Epiphany: Discovering the Essence of Bourbon

The moment Di Tran first sipped Buffalo Trace George T. Stagg was nothing short of an epiphany. This was no ordinary drink; it was bourbon in its purest form—barrel-proof, undiluted, and unapologetically strong. The experience was unlike

Kentucky Bourbon: The Pride of the Bluegrass State
Di Tran Bourbon BELIEF: Bridging American Bourbon to the World

anything he had ever encountered with Cognac. The high proof of the bourbon, combined with its complex flavors, left an indelible mark on Di Tran. It was as if he had finally understood what bourbon truly represented—a spirit that was not just about drinking, but about savoring, appreciating, and connecting.

For Di Tran, this moment was more than just a tasting experience; it was a revelation. He realized that bourbon, like life, was best experienced in its most authentic form. The richness of the barrel-proof bourbon, untouched by water, symbolized a purity and strength that resonated deeply with him. It was in this moment that the seeds of Di Tran Bourbon BELIEF were planted.

Bourbon and the Kentucky Way of Life

As Di Tran delved deeper into the world of bourbon, he came to appreciate the intricate relationship between this spirit and the Kentucky way of life. Bourbon was more than just a drink; it was a reflection of the state's culture, its history, and its people. Kentucky, with its unique climate and limestone-rich water, provided the perfect environment for bourbon making. But it was the people, with their dedication to craftsmanship and tradition, who made Kentucky bourbon what it is today.

Kentucky Bourbon: The Pride of the Bluegrass State
Di Tran Bourbon BELIEF: Bridging American Bourbon to the World

Di Tran began to see bourbon as a metaphor for his own journey. Just as bourbon is aged and refined over time, so too was he being shaped by his experiences in Kentucky. The love and care he received from the people around him, the community that embraced him, all contributed to his growth and transformation. Bourbon became a symbol of this journey—a spirit that, like him, was "Vietnamese Born and American Made."

The Birth of Di Tran Bourbon BELIEF

The creation of Di Tran Bourbon BELIEF was the culmination of this journey. Inspired by his experiences and the principles he had come to hold dear, Di Tran set out to create a bourbon that embodied the values of authenticity, strength, and connection. He wanted to craft a bourbon that was straight from the barrel, undiluted and strong, yet aged to perfection—a bourbon that would bring people together in the same way that Kentucky had brought him into its fold.

Di Tran Bourbon BELIEF is more than just a spirit; it is a philosophy. It represents the belief that life is best lived authentically, without dilution or compromise. The 8-year aging process ensures that the bourbon is rich in flavor, smooth in texture, and powerful in its impact. But more than that, it is a bourbon that is

Kentucky Bourbon: The Pride of the Bluegrass State
Di Tran Bourbon BELIEF: Bridging American Bourbon to the World

meant to be shared—with family, friends, and loved ones. It is a drink for those who appreciate the finer things in life, not just for their material value, but for the connections they foster and the memories they create.

Savoring the Moment: Bourbon as a Connector

For Di Tran, bourbon is more than just a drink; it is a bridge. It is a way to connect with others, to share stories, and to build relationships. Whether it is sipped slowly on a quiet evening after a long day, or shared among friends during a celebration, bourbon has the power to bring people together. This is the essence of Di Tran Bourbon BELIEF—a spirit that not only reflects the strength and authenticity of Kentucky bourbon but also embodies the values of love, care, and human connection.

As Di Tran reflects on his journey, from a young immigrant in a new land to a successful entrepreneur and bourbon maker, he sees the parallels between his life and the bourbon he has come to love. Both have been shaped by time, by the people who have influenced them, and by the environments in which they have grown. And both, in their own way, represent the belief that the best things in life are those that are lived authentically and shared with others.

Kentucky Bourbon: The Pride of the Bluegrass State
Di Tran Bourbon BELIEF: Bridging American Bourbon to the World

Conclusion: A Legacy of Belief

The introduction of Di Tran Bourbon BELIEF marks a new chapter in Di Tran's life, one that is deeply rooted in the values he has come to cherish. It is a tribute to the state that welcomed him, the people who supported him, and the spirit that inspired him. But more than that, it is a testament to the power of belief—the belief that anything is possible when you stay true to yourself, your values, and your community.

As you hold a bottle of Di Tran Bourbon BELIEF in your hands, you are not just holding a drink; you are holding a piece of Di Tran's journey, a symbol of the love, care, and connection that Kentucky bourbon represents. It is a drink that is meant to be shared, to bring people together, and to celebrate the moments that make life meaningful. In every sip, you will taste the essence of Kentucky, the strength of its spirit, and the belief that brought it all to life.

Chapter 1: The Heart of Kentucky – A Legacy of Bourbon

The Birth of Bourbon: A Legacy Rooted in Time

The story of Kentucky bourbon begins long before Di Tran Bourbon BELIEF ever graced the shelves. It is a

Kentucky Bourbon: The Pride of the Bluegrass State
Di Tran Bourbon BELIEF: Bridging American Bourbon to the World

tale that dates back to the late 18th century, a time when settlers were first drawn to Kentucky's fertile land. The year was 1789 when the Reverend Elijah Craig, often credited as the inventor of bourbon, began producing whiskey in the rolling hills of Kentucky. Craig's whiskey was unique; it was made from a grain mixture of at least 51% corn, distilled and aged in charred oak barrels, giving it a distinctive flavor that would eventually become synonymous with the Bluegrass State.

Kentucky's terrain, with its limestone-rich soil and abundant natural springs, provided the perfect conditions for growing corn and producing whiskey. The limestone filtered the water, making it rich in calcium and iron-free, ideal for whiskey production. Over the years, the practice of distilling whiskey in Kentucky grew, and by the early 19th century, bourbon had established itself as the drink of choice across America.

The Role of Corn: The Golden Grain of Bourbon

Corn, often referred to as "Kentucky gold," plays a pivotal role in bourbon production. The state's climate and soil make it an ideal location for growing this grain, which is why it became the primary ingredient in bourbon. The use of corn gives bourbon its

Kentucky Bourbon: The Pride of the Bluegrass State
Di Tran Bourbon BELIEF: Bridging American Bourbon to the World

characteristic sweetness, setting it apart from other whiskies. By law, bourbon must be made from at least 51% corn, though many distilleries, including those that produce Di Tran Bourbon BELIEF, use a higher percentage to achieve a richer flavor.

The importance of corn in bourbon production cannot be overstated. It is the backbone of the spirit, providing the base for the mash that is distilled and aged to perfection. Kentucky's commitment to quality corn production is evident in the care and attention given to the farming and selection of this vital ingredient. From seed to harvest, every step is meticulously managed to ensure that only the finest corn is used in the production of bourbon.

The Evolution of Kentucky Bourbon

As the 19th century progressed, bourbon production in Kentucky continued to flourish. By the mid-1800s, bourbon had become a major industry in the state, with hundreds of distilleries operating across the region. These early distillers, many of whom were farmers by trade, perfected the art of bourbon making, passing down their techniques from generation to generation.

The Civil War brought challenges to the bourbon industry, but it also highlighted the spirit's resilience. Even during times of hardship, Kentucky distillers

Kentucky Bourbon: The Pride of the Bluegrass State
Di Tran Bourbon BELIEF: Bridging American Bourbon to the World

remained committed to their craft, producing bourbon that was sought after by soldiers and civilians alike. The end of the war saw a resurgence in bourbon production, with Kentucky firmly establishing itself as the epicenter of American whiskey.

The Rise of Iconic Distilleries

The late 19th and early 20th centuries were a golden age for Kentucky bourbon. It was during this time that many of the state's most iconic distilleries were founded, distilleries that remain household names today. Names like Jim Beam, Maker's Mark, Wild Turkey, and Buffalo Trace began to emerge as leaders in the industry, each contributing to the rich tapestry of Kentucky bourbon.

Buffalo Trace, in particular, holds a special place in the heart of bourbon enthusiasts. Founded in 1775, Buffalo Trace is one of the oldest continuously operating distilleries in America. It has survived wars, Prohibition, and economic downturns, emerging each time stronger and more revered. Buffalo Trace is also the distillery where Di Tran Bourbon BELIEF finds its roots, a fact that ties Di Tran's story to the very heart of Kentucky's bourbon legacy.

Today, these distilleries, along with others like Woodford Reserve, Four Roses, Heaven Hill, and

Kentucky Bourbon: The Pride of the Bluegrass State
Di Tran Bourbon BELIEF: Bridging American Bourbon to the World

Bulleit, form the backbone of Kentucky's bourbon industry. Each distillery has its own unique story, its own traditions, and its own approach to making bourbon, but all share a common commitment to quality and heritage.

Di Tran Bourbon BELIEF: A New Chapter in Kentucky's Story

The creation of Di Tran Bourbon BELIEF is a testament to the enduring legacy of Kentucky bourbon. Crafted in Louisville's Beechmont neighborhood, Di Tran Bourbon BELIEF is a celebration of the state's rich history and its unwavering commitment to excellence. The decision to partner with a distillery as renowned as Buffalo Trace speaks to the care and attention that Di Tran has poured into this project.

Di Tran Bourbon BELIEF is aged for eight years, a period that allows the bourbon to develop its full character and complexity. The aging process is crucial, as the bourbon takes on the flavors of the charred oak barrels in which it is stored. Over time, the bourbon absorbs the caramelized sugars from the wood, resulting in a drink that is rich, smooth, and full-bodied. This attention to detail is what sets Di Tran Bourbon BELIEF apart, ensuring that each bottle is a

Kentucky Bourbon: The Pride of the Bluegrass State
Di Tran Bourbon BELIEF: Bridging American Bourbon to the World

true reflection of Kentucky's bourbon-making tradition.

The Top 10 Distilleries in Kentucky Today

Kentucky is home to some of the world's most famous distilleries, and the state's bourbon trail is a pilgrimage for whiskey lovers. Here are the top 10 distilleries that continue to define Kentucky bourbon:

1. **Buffalo Trace Distillery** - As one of the oldest distilleries in America, Buffalo Trace is a leader in the bourbon industry, producing a range of highly sought-after whiskeys, including the legendary George T. Stagg.

2. **Jim Beam Distillery** - Founded in 1795, Jim Beam is perhaps the most recognizable name in bourbon, known for its extensive portfolio of whiskeys.

3. **Maker's Mark Distillery** - Maker's Mark is famous for its red wax-sealed bottles and its smooth, wheat-based bourbon, which has garnered a loyal following worldwide.

4. **Wild Turkey Distillery** - Located in Lawrenceburg, Wild Turkey is known for its bold, high-proof bourbons that pack a punch without sacrificing flavor.

Kentucky Bourbon: The Pride of the Bluegrass State
Di Tran Bourbon BELIEF: Bridging American Bourbon to the World

5. **Woodford Reserve Distillery** - Woodford Reserve is celebrated for its artisanal approach to bourbon making, producing small-batch whiskeys that are refined and elegant.

6. **Four Roses Distillery** - Four Roses is unique in its use of ten distinct bourbon recipes, resulting in a versatile and award-winning range of products.

7. **Heaven Hill Distillery** - Heaven Hill is the largest independent, family-owned and operated distillery in America, producing iconic brands like Elijah Craig and Larceny.

8. **Bulleit Distillery** - Bulleit is known for its high-rye bourbon and innovative approach to whiskey making, appealing to both traditionalists and newcomers alike.

9. **Old Forester Distillery** - As the first bourbon sold exclusively in sealed bottles, Old Forester has a long history of quality and consistency.

10. **Angel's Envy Distillery** - Angel's Envy is a newer distillery, but it has quickly made a name for itself with its unique bourbon finished in port wine barrels.

Kentucky Bourbon: The Pride of the Bluegrass State
Di Tran Bourbon BELIEF: Bridging American Bourbon to the World

These distilleries represent the pinnacle of bourbon production in Kentucky, each contributing to the state's reputation as the bourbon capital of the world.

The Spirit of Kentucky: More Than Just a Drink

To understand bourbon is to understand Kentucky itself. The spirit of Kentucky bourbon is woven into the fabric of the state's culture, its economy, and its way of life. It represents the values of hard work, resilience, and a deep respect for tradition. But more than that, bourbon is about community. It is a drink that brings people together, whether it's at a distillery tour, a local bar, or a family gathering.

Bourbon has a way of breaking down barriers, of creating connections between people from all walks of life. It's a drink that encourages conversation, fosters friendships, and builds bonds that last a lifetime. This is the spirit that Di Tran Bourbon BELIEF seeks to capture—a spirit of connection, of shared experiences, and of belief in something greater than oneself.

The Beechmont Neighborhood: A Place of Belief

Louisville's Beechmont neighborhood, where Di Tran Bourbon BELIEF is crafted, is a place that embodies the diversity and vibrancy of Kentucky. It's a community that has welcomed people from all over the

Kentucky Bourbon: The Pride of the Bluegrass State
Di Tran Bourbon BELIEF: Bridging American Bourbon to the World

world, each bringing their own traditions and cultures. This melting pot of influences is what makes Beechmont so special, and it's this spirit of inclusion and community that Di Tran has sought to infuse into his bourbon.

Di Tran Bourbon BELIEF is not just a product of Kentucky; it is a product of Beechmont, a neighborhood that has become a second home for Di Tran. The bourbon is a reflection of the values that the community holds dear—authenticity, strength, and a commitment to quality. It is a bourbon that is meant to be shared, to bring people together, and to celebrate the moments that matter most.

Conclusion: A Legacy of Love and Pride

The story of Kentucky bourbon is a story of love and pride—love for the craft of bourbon making, and pride in the heritage that has been passed down through generations. Di Tran Bourbon BELIEF is a continuation of this legacy, a bourbon that honors the traditions of the past while looking towards the future.

As you sip Di Tran Bourbon BELIEF, you are not just tasting a drink; you are tasting a piece of Kentucky's history. You are experiencing the love and care that has gone into every bottle, the pride that comes from being a part of something bigger than oneself. It is a

Kentucky Bourbon: The Pride of the Bluegrass State
Di Tran Bourbon BELIEF: Bridging American Bourbon to the World

legacy that will continue to be passed down, one sip at a time, from generation to generation.

In the heart of Kentucky, where the rolling hills meet the bluegrass, and where bourbon is more than just a drink, Di Tran Bourbon BELIEF stands as a testament to the enduring spirit of this great state. It is a bourbon that is "Vietnamese Born and American Made," a symbol of the belief that anything is possible when you stay true to your roots, your values, and your community.

Kentucky Bourbon: The Pride of the Bluegrass State
Di Tran Bourbon BELIEF: Bridging American Bourbon to the World

Chapter 2: Kentucky Bourbon – A Class of Its Own

The Unmatched Legacy of Kentucky Bourbon

Kentucky bourbon is more than just a drink; it is an embodiment of the state's rich heritage, a symbol of craftsmanship, and a testament to time-honored traditions. In a world awash with spirits of every kind—ranging from the refined elegance of French Cognac to the bold, peaty notes of Scottish and Irish whiskey, the vibrant, tropical notes of Caribbean rum, and the crisp, neutral tones of vodka—Kentucky bourbon stands in a class of its own. Its distinctive character, shaped by Kentucky's unique climate, limestone-filtered water, and centuries of meticulous craftsmanship, has elevated it to a position of global acclaim.

As a spirit, bourbon is quintessentially American, yet its appeal transcends borders. In recent years, Kentucky bourbon has not only maintained its status as a domestic favorite but has also made significant inroads into the global market. The rise of bourbon, particularly high-proof, aged bourbons like Di Tran Bourbon BELIEF, has captured the attention of connoisseurs worldwide. This chapter explores how Kentucky bourbon has distinguished itself on the

Kentucky Bourbon: The Pride of the Bluegrass State
Di Tran Bourbon BELIEF: Bridging American Bourbon to the World

global stage, emphasizing its smoothness, strength, and the powerful sensory experience it offers—a drink that is smooth yet potent, with a complexity that only comes from careful aging.

The Distinctive Qualities of Kentucky Bourbon

The distinct character of Kentucky bourbon is rooted in several key factors that set it apart from other spirits. First and foremost is the grain bill. Bourbon must be made from a mash that contains at least 51% corn, a requirement that gives the spirit its signature sweetness. The rest of the mash is typically composed of rye or wheat and malted barley, each contributing to the bourbon's flavor profile. This combination of grains is then fermented, distilled, and aged in new charred oak barrels, where it gains complexity and depth over time.

Kentucky's climate plays a crucial role in this aging process. The state experiences hot summers and cold winters, causing the bourbon to expand and contract within the barrels. This movement allows the spirit to absorb the flavors of the charred oak, imparting notes of caramel, vanilla, and spice that are characteristic of well-aged bourbon. The limestone-filtered water, abundant in Kentucky, is another essential element. Rich in calcium and iron-free, this water is ideal for

Kentucky Bourbon: The Pride of the Bluegrass State
Di Tran Bourbon BELIEF: Bridging American Bourbon to the World

whiskey production, giving Kentucky bourbon a purity and smoothness that is hard to replicate elsewhere.

The aging process is where bourbon truly comes into its own. Unlike many other spirits that may be bottled relatively young, bourbon is often aged for several years, allowing it to develop a complexity that is both deep and nuanced. Di Tran Bourbon BELIEF, aged for eight years, exemplifies this principle. The extended aging period allows the bourbon to mellow, smoothing out any rough edges while intensifying its flavor profile. The result is a spirit that is rich, smooth, and incredibly satisfying, with a powerful kick that is both warming and invigorating.

Kentucky Bourbon on the Global Stage

In recent years, Kentucky bourbon has experienced a renaissance on the global stage. What was once seen as a distinctly American drink has now captured the attention of international markets, with bourbon exports reaching record highs. This surge in popularity can be attributed to several factors, including the growing global interest in craft spirits, the increasing appreciation for high-quality, aged products, and the unique story that bourbon tells—a story of heritage, craftsmanship, and authenticity.

Kentucky Bourbon: The Pride of the Bluegrass State
Di Tran Bourbon BELIEF: Bridging American Bourbon to the World

As global consumers seek out premium spirits, Kentucky bourbon has emerged as a top contender. The complexity and depth of aged bourbon, particularly those with higher proofs like Di Tran Bourbon BELIEF, have resonated with drinkers who appreciate a spirit that offers more than just a simple sip. Bourbon's ability to deliver a rich, multi-layered experience, with notes ranging from sweet to spicy, and its smooth yet strong finish, have made it a favorite among those who seek a drink that engages all the senses.

One of the key aspects of bourbon's global appeal is its versatility. While bourbon is traditionally enjoyed neat or on the rocks, its robust flavor profile makes it an excellent base for cocktails, both classic and modern. This adaptability has helped bourbon find its way into bars and homes across the world, where it is celebrated for its ability to enhance a wide range of drinks. From the Old Fashioned to the Manhattan, bourbon's influence is felt in some of the most iconic cocktails, further solidifying its status as a global spirit.

The Sensory Experience of Bourbon

To truly appreciate Kentucky bourbon, one must understand the sensory experience it offers. Bourbon is not just about taste; it is about the full-bodied

Kentucky Bourbon: The Pride of the Bluegrass State
Di Tran Bourbon BELIEF: Bridging American Bourbon to the World

experience that begins with the first pour and continues with each sip. The color of bourbon, a deep amber hue, speaks to its time spent in charred oak barrels, where it takes on the rich tones of caramel and toffee. This visual appeal is the first indication of the depth that lies within the glass.

The aroma of bourbon is equally telling. When a glass of Di Tran Bourbon BELIEF is lifted to the nose, it reveals a bouquet of scents—vanilla, caramel, oak, and a hint of spice. These aromas are a prelude to the complex flavors that follow, inviting the drinker to explore the nuances that have developed over years of aging.

But it is the taste and the feel of bourbon that truly set it apart. A sip of Di Tran Bourbon BELIEF begins with a smooth, sweet entry, where the flavors of corn, caramel, and vanilla are immediately apparent. As the bourbon moves across the palate, it reveals layers of complexity—hints of dried fruit, toasted nuts, and a gentle spice that adds warmth without overwhelming the senses. The high proof of the bourbon delivers a powerful kick, a reminder of its strength and the care with which it has been crafted.

As the bourbon is swallowed, it leaves behind a lingering warmth that spreads from the throat to the

Kentucky Bourbon: The Pride of the Bluegrass State
Di Tran Bourbon BELIEF: Bridging American Bourbon to the World

chest, a sensation that is both comforting and invigorating. This finish, often described as a "Kentucky hug," is one of the defining characteristics of a good bourbon. It is a reminder that bourbon is not just a drink to be consumed quickly, but a spirit to be savored, to be enjoyed slowly as it reveals its full character.

Bourbon's Global Influence

Kentucky bourbon's rise on the global stage is not just a testament to its quality but also to its cultural significance. As more people around the world discover bourbon, they are also discovering a piece of American heritage. Bourbon tells the story of a nation, of its frontier spirit, its dedication to craftsmanship, and its commitment to quality. This narrative resonates with consumers who are increasingly looking for products with a story, products that offer more than just a fleeting experience.

In markets like Europe and Asia, bourbon has gained a significant following. In countries with a long tradition of whiskey drinking, such as Scotland and Ireland, bourbon is seen as a bold alternative—something familiar yet different, offering a new twist on an old favorite. In countries like Japan, where whiskey culture is deeply ingrained, bourbon has found a place among

Kentucky Bourbon: The Pride of the Bluegrass State
Di Tran Bourbon BELIEF: Bridging American Bourbon to the World

discerning drinkers who appreciate its complexity and depth.

The global appeal of bourbon is also evident in the growing number of international awards it has received. Competitions like the San Francisco World Spirits Competition and the International Wine & Spirit Competition have recognized Kentucky bourbon for its excellence, further cementing its status as a world-class spirit. Di Tran Bourbon BELIEF, with its 8-year aging process and high proof, stands as a proud representative of this tradition, bringing the best of Kentucky to a global audience.

The Kick of Kentucky Bourbon

One of the most distinctive qualities of Kentucky bourbon, particularly high-proof varieties like Di Tran Bourbon BELIEF, is the powerful kick it delivers. This kick is not just about the alcohol content, but about the way the bourbon engages the senses. It is the combination of smoothness and strength, of sweetness and spice, that creates a drink that is both approachable and formidable.

Di Tran often describes this experience as a revelation. Growing up with spirits like Cognac XO, he was accustomed to a certain elegance in drinking—a smooth, refined experience that was pleasant but not

Kentucky Bourbon: The Pride of the Bluegrass State
Di Tran Bourbon BELIEF: Bridging American Bourbon to the World

necessarily powerful. Bourbon, however, was different. The first time Di Tran tasted a high-proof bourbon, he was struck by its intensity. The smooth entry was familiar, but it was followed by a burst of flavor and a fiery warmth that was entirely new. This was not just a drink; it was an experience.

The kick of bourbon is part of what makes it so special. It is a reminder that this is a spirit with character, a drink that has been shaped by time and tradition. It is a drink that demands respect, one that should be savored slowly, allowing the flavors to unfold and the warmth to spread. This kick is also what makes bourbon so satisfying. It is a drink that can stand on its own, one that does not need to be masked by mixers or diluted by water.

The Smoothness of Aged Bourbon

While the kick of bourbon is a defining feature, so too is its smoothness. This may seem contradictory, but it is the balance of these two qualities that makes bourbon so unique. The smoothness of bourbon comes from its aging process, where the spirit spends years in charred oak barrels, mellowing and developing its complex flavor profile.

For Di Tran Bourbon BELIEF, this smoothness is the result of eight years of careful aging. During this time,

Kentucky Bourbon: The Pride of the Bluegrass State
Di Tran Bourbon BELIEF: Bridging American Bourbon to the World

the bourbon interacts with the wood, absorbing flavors of caramel, vanilla, and spice, while also losing some of its harsher edges. The result is a drink that is rich and full-bodied, yet smooth enough to be enjoyed neat.

This smoothness is what allows bourbon to be so versatile. It can be sipped slowly, savored for its complexity, or it can be the base of a cocktail, adding depth and richness to the drink. But no matter how it is enjoyed, the smoothness of bourbon is always present, a testament to the care and craftsmanship that go into every bottle.

The Global Future of Kentucky Bourbon

As Kentucky bourbon continues to gain popularity around the world, its future looks brighter than ever. With more people discovering the joy of bourbon, the demand for high-quality, aged products like Di Tran Bourbon BELIEF is only going to increase. This is a spirit that has proven itself on the global stage, one that offers a unique combination of tradition and innovation, of strength and smoothness.

The global market for bourbon is growing, with new markets opening up in countries like China, India, and Brazil. As these markets mature, the appreciation for premium spirits will only continue to rise, and Kentucky bourbon is poised to be at the forefront of

Kentucky Bourbon: The Pride of the Bluegrass State
Di Tran Bourbon BELIEF: Bridging American Bourbon to the World

this trend. For Di Tran, this is an exciting time. His bourbon, crafted with love and pride in Kentucky, is now reaching a global audience, sharing the story of Kentucky with the world.

In conclusion, Kentucky bourbon is truly a class of its own. It is a spirit that combines the best of American tradition with the complexity and depth that come from years of careful aging. Di Tran Bourbon BELIEF, with its high proof and smooth finish, is a prime example of what makes Kentucky bourbon so special. It is a drink that is meant to be savored, to be enjoyed with friends and loved ones, and to be appreciated for the rich history and craftsmanship that go into every bottle. As bourbon continues to make its mark on the global stage, it is clear that Kentucky's gift to the world is here to stay.

Kentucky Bourbon: The Pride of the Bluegrass State
Di Tran Bourbon BELIEF: Bridging American Bourbon to the World

Chapter 3: BELIEF – More Than a Drink

The Essence of BELIEF: A Philosophy in a Bottle

Di Tran Bourbon BELIEF is not just a drink; it is a manifestation of a philosophy, a symbol of trust, unity, and the power of human connection. From the moment the idea of Di Tran Bourbon BELIEF was conceived, it was clear that this would be no ordinary bourbon. It would be a spirit that transcends the simple act of drinking, becoming instead a catalyst for meaningful interactions, deep conversations, and lasting bonds.

The decision to bottle this bourbon straight from the barrel, without dilution, was not merely a production choice; it was a declaration. It was a statement of authenticity, a belief that the best things in life should be experienced in their purest form. This commitment to authenticity reflects a deeper understanding that in a world often filled with pretense and superficiality, there is immense value in things that are genuine—whether it's the bourbon we drink or the relationships we cultivate.

BELIEF is about more than just the bourbon itself; it's about the moments that are created when people come together to share it. It's about lowering our guards,

Kentucky Bourbon: The Pride of the Bluegrass State
Di Tran Bourbon BELIEF: Bridging American Bourbon to the World

allowing ourselves to be vulnerable, and building connections that are as strong and lasting as the bourbon in our glasses.

The New Culture of Di Tran Bourbon BELIEF

In today's fast-paced world, where instant gratification often takes precedence over quality and depth, Di Tran Bourbon BELIEF seeks to carve out a different path. This bourbon is not meant to be consumed quickly or mindlessly; it is meant to be savored, to be appreciated slowly, with intention and care. The culture that surrounds Di Tran Bourbon BELIEF is one of connection, bonding, and sharing—values that are embodied in every sip.

This culture is rooted in the idea that bourbon, particularly a bourbon as carefully crafted as Di Tran Bourbon BELIEF, is best enjoyed in the company of others. Whether you are sitting down with family, gathering with friends, or negotiating with business partners, sharing a glass of bourbon can create a space for open and honest conversation. It can transform a casual meeting into a memorable occasion, a simple gathering into a moment of genuine connection.

The culture of Di Tran Bourbon BELIEF is one where the act of drinking bourbon becomes a ritual of sorts—a way to mark important moments, to celebrate

Kentucky Bourbon: The Pride of the Bluegrass State
Di Tran Bourbon BELIEF: Bridging American Bourbon to the World

successes, and to deepen relationships. It is about more than just enjoying the taste of a fine spirit; it is about the shared experience, the stories told, and the bonds formed over a glass of bourbon that has been aged for eight years to achieve its full potential.

The Power of Sipping, Not Drinking

One of the key principles of the Di Tran Bourbon BELIEF culture is the idea of sipping, not drinking. This may seem like a small distinction, but it is one that carries significant weight. To drink something is to consume it quickly, often without much thought. To sip, on the other hand, is to take your time, to appreciate the nuances of flavor, and to allow the experience to unfold gradually.

When you sip Di Tran Bourbon BELIEF, you are engaging with the bourbon in a way that honors the craftsmanship that went into its creation. You are allowing the flavors to develop on your palate, from the initial sweetness of the corn to the rich, complex notes of caramel, vanilla, and spice that come from years spent aging in charred oak barrels. Each sip is an opportunity to discover something new, to experience the bourbon in a deeper, more meaningful way.

Sipping also allows you to fully experience the strength of the bourbon. Di Tran Bourbon BELIEF is

Kentucky Bourbon: The Pride of the Bluegrass State
Di Tran Bourbon BELIEF: Bridging American Bourbon to the World

bottled at barrel proof, which means it is strong—both in flavor and in alcohol content. When you sip it, you feel the warmth as it goes down, the way it burns slightly in your throat, and the way it spreads a comforting warmth throughout your chest. This is not a harsh burn, but a reminder of the power and complexity of the spirit you are drinking.

The Art of Conversation: Bonding Over Bourbon

Bourbon has always been a social drink, one that brings people together in a way that few other spirits can. There is something about sharing a glass of bourbon that invites conversation, that encourages people to open up and share their thoughts, their stories, and their experiences. This is particularly true of Di Tran Bourbon BELIEF, a bourbon that is designed to be shared in moments of connection and camaraderie.

In the culture of Di Tran Bourbon BELIEF, conversation is an essential part of the experience. It is during these moments of shared conversation that bonds are formed, trust is built, and relationships are strengthened. Whether you are discussing business, reflecting on life, or simply enjoying each other's company, the act of sharing a glass of bourbon creates a space where meaningful dialogue can take place.

Kentucky Bourbon: The Pride of the Bluegrass State
Di Tran Bourbon BELIEF: Bridging American Bourbon to the World

This is why Di Tran Bourbon BELIEF is more than just a drink; it is a tool for building connections. It is a way to create moments of intimacy and understanding, to deepen relationships and to create memories that will last long after the bourbon has been finished. In a world where so much of our communication is superficial and fleeting, the conversations that take place over a glass of Di Tran Bourbon BELIEF are a reminder of the value of real, genuine human connection.

The Beauty of the Buzz

One of the most enjoyable aspects of drinking bourbon, particularly a high-proof bourbon like Di Tran Bourbon BELIEF, is the buzz that comes with it. This buzz is not about getting drunk; it is about reaching a state of relaxation and contentment, where the stresses of the day begin to fade away, and the conversation flows more easily. It is about finding that sweet spot where the bourbon has softened the edges of your thoughts, making everything just a little bit more enjoyable.

The buzz of Di Tran Bourbon BELIEF is a gentle one, a gradual warmth that spreads through your body, making you feel at ease. It is a reminder to slow down, to take your time, and to enjoy the moment. This is

Kentucky Bourbon: The Pride of the Bluegrass State
Di Tran Bourbon BELIEF: Bridging American Bourbon to the World

why the culture of Di Tran Bourbon BELIEF emphasizes sipping—because it is not about how much you drink, but about how much you enjoy the experience.

As the buzz sets in, you begin to appreciate the nuances of the bourbon even more. The flavors become richer, the warmth more comforting, and the conversation more meaningful. This is the magic of Di Tran Bourbon BELIEF—it enhances the moment without overpowering it, allowing you to fully engage with the people around you and the experience you are sharing.

Conversations of Value: Adding Depth to Every Interaction

In the culture of Di Tran Bourbon BELIEF, conversations are not just idle chatter; they are opportunities to add value, to deepen understanding, and to explore the beauty of the world around us. Whether you are discussing business strategies, reflecting on personal growth, or sharing stories of past experiences, the conversations that take place over a glass of bourbon are enriched by the depth and complexity of the spirit itself.

Di Tran Bourbon BELIEF is a bourbon that encourages you to think deeply, to reflect on the things

Kentucky Bourbon: The Pride of the Bluegrass State
Di Tran Bourbon BELIEF: Bridging American Bourbon to the World

that matter most, and to engage with others in a way that is both meaningful and rewarding. It is a bourbon that is meant to be enjoyed in moments of introspection and in conversations that go beyond the surface. This is why it is so well-suited to being shared with business partners, friends, and loved ones—because it has the ability to add depth and richness to any interaction.

These conversations of value are what make the experience of drinking Di Tran Bourbon BELIEF so special. They are a reminder that the best moments in life are the ones that are shared, the ones where we connect with others on a deeper level, and the ones where we take the time to truly appreciate the beauty of the world around us.

The Ritual of Sharing: A New Tradition

In many cultures, the act of sharing a drink is a ritual, a way to honor relationships and to celebrate the bonds that connect us. Di Tran Bourbon BELIEF is designed to be a part of this tradition, a bourbon that is meant to be shared and enjoyed with others. Whether you are raising a glass to celebrate a milestone, to mark a special occasion, or simply to enjoy each other's company, Di Tran Bourbon BELIEF is the perfect companion.

Kentucky Bourbon: The Pride of the Bluegrass State
Di Tran Bourbon BELIEF: Bridging American Bourbon to the World

The ritual of sharing Di Tran Bourbon BELIEF is one that is steeped in respect for the spirit itself, as well as for the people with whom you are sharing it. It is a ritual that emphasizes the importance of taking your time, of savoring each sip, and of engaging fully with the moment. It is a ritual that honors the craftsmanship that went into making the bourbon, as well as the relationships that are being celebrated.

This tradition of sharing is at the heart of the Di Tran Bourbon BELIEF culture. It is a way to create new memories, to strengthen old bonds, and to build new connections. It is a way to bring people together in a spirit of unity and trust, and to celebrate the things that matter most in life.

The Beauty of the World: Reflecting on Life with Bourbon in Hand

There is something about sipping bourbon that invites reflection. As you sit with a glass of Di Tran Bourbon BELIEF in your hand, the world seems to slow down, allowing you to take a step back and appreciate the beauty of life. Whether it's the warmth of the bourbon, the depth of its flavors, or the connection you feel with the people around you, this is a moment to reflect on the things that make life truly meaningful.

Kentucky Bourbon: The Pride of the Bluegrass State
Di Tran Bourbon BELIEF: Bridging American Bourbon to the World

In these moments of reflection, bourbon becomes more than just a drink; it becomes a lens through which you can see the world more clearly. It is a reminder to appreciate the small things, to find joy in the simple pleasures, and to recognize the beauty that exists all around us. This is the power of Di Tran Bourbon BELIEF—it enhances your ability to see the world in a way that is richer, deeper, and more connected.

These moments of reflection are what make the experience of drinking Di Tran Bourbon BELIEF so special. They are a reminder that life is about more than just getting through the day; it is about finding meaning, creating connections, and appreciating the beauty that exists in every moment.

BELIEF: A Legacy of Connection and Trust

Di Tran Bourbon BELIEF is more than just a drink; it is a legacy. It is a symbol of the values that Di Tran holds dear—authenticity, connection, and trust. It is a bourbon that is meant to be shared, to bring people together, and to create moments of genuine connection. In a world that often values speed and convenience over quality and depth, Di Tran Bourbon BELIEF is a reminder that the best things in life are worth taking the time to savor.

Kentucky Bourbon: The Pride of the Bluegrass State
Di Tran Bourbon BELIEF: Bridging American Bourbon to the World

As you share a glass of Di Tran Bourbon BELIEF with family, friends, or business partners, you are not just enjoying a fine bourbon; you are participating in a tradition of connection and trust. You are creating memories that will last a lifetime, building relationships that are based on mutual respect, and celebrating the things that make life truly meaningful.

This is the legacy of Di Tran Bourbon BELIEF—a legacy of connection, of trust, and of belief in the power of human connection. It is a legacy that will continue to be passed down, one sip at a time, from generation to generation. And as you raise your glass, you can take pride in knowing that you are part of something greater, something that is more than just a drink, but a symbol of the things that truly matter in life.

Chapter 4: The Cultural Tapestry of Kentucky

A Land of Four Seasons: Heaven on Earth

Kentucky Bourbon: The Pride of the Bluegrass State
Di Tran Bourbon BELIEF: Bridging American Bourbon to the World

For Di Tran, coming from the tropical climes of Vietnam, Kentucky represents a kind of paradise, a place where the natural beauty and seasonal changes are nothing short of awe-inspiring. Unlike the perpetual warmth and humidity of Vietnam, Kentucky is a land where the year is divided into four distinct seasons, each bringing its own unique charm and influence. This cyclical dance of nature is not just a backdrop to life in Kentucky; it is a fundamental part of the state's culture and identity, shaping everything from the way people live to the way bourbon is made.

In Kentucky, the seasons unfold with a rhythmic precision, each lasting about three to four months. Spring breathes life into the land with a riot of colors and fresh blooms, symbolizing renewal and hope. Summer follows with its warm embrace, filling the air with the sounds of cicadas and the scent of flowering gardens. Autumn arrives with a spectacular display of reds, oranges, and yellows, as the leaves turn and the air becomes crisp. Finally, winter blankets the state in a serene stillness, the cold air sharp and invigorating, a time for reflection and warmth by the fire.

For Di Tran, the experience of these seasons is a revelation, a reminder of the beauty and diversity that nature has to offer. In Vietnam, where the climate is relatively consistent year-round, the concept of four

Kentucky Bourbon: The Pride of the Bluegrass State
Di Tran Bourbon BELIEF: Bridging American Bourbon to the World

distinct seasons was something he had only read about in books. But in Kentucky, he found himself living it, experiencing firsthand the profound impact that the changing seasons have on both the land and the people.

The Impact of Seasons on Bourbon Aging

The beauty of Kentucky's four seasons is not just a visual or sensory experience; it plays a crucial role in the process of bourbon aging. Unlike other spirits, bourbon is uniquely affected by the fluctuations in temperature and humidity that come with the changing seasons. This is particularly true in Kentucky, where the climate can range from the sweltering heat of summer to the bitter cold of winter, with temperatures varying from as high as 120 degrees Fahrenheit to as low as -5 degrees.

These temperature extremes cause the bourbon to expand and contract within the barrels, pushing the liquid in and out of the charred oak staves. This process allows the bourbon to absorb the rich flavors of the wood, imparting notes of caramel, vanilla, and spice that are characteristic of well-aged bourbon. The hot summers accelerate the interaction between the bourbon and the wood, while the cold winters slow it down, allowing the spirit to mellow and develop complexity over time.

Kentucky Bourbon: The Pride of the Bluegrass State
Di Tran Bourbon BELIEF: Bridging American Bourbon to the World

In this way, the seasons are not just a backdrop to the bourbon-making process; they are an active participant, contributing to the unique flavor profile of each batch. Di Tran Bourbon BELIEF, with its 8-year aging process, is a perfect example of how Kentucky's climate shapes the character of the bourbon. Each bottle carries with it the essence of Kentucky's seasons—the warmth of summer, the richness of autumn, the depth of winter, and the renewal of spring.

The Ohio River: A Lifeblood of Kentucky

The Ohio River, winding its way through the heart of Kentucky, is more than just a geographic feature; it is a lifeblood that has sustained the people and the culture of the region for centuries. The river has been a source of transportation, trade, and sustenance, shaping the history and development of Kentucky in countless ways. But perhaps one of its most significant contributions is the role it plays in the bourbon industry.

The water of the Ohio River, filtered through Kentucky's limestone foundation, is exceptionally pure and rich in minerals. This limestone acts as a natural filter, removing impurities such as iron, which can impart unwanted flavors to the bourbon, while adding calcium, which is beneficial for fermentation. The

Kentucky Bourbon: The Pride of the Bluegrass State
Di Tran Bourbon BELIEF: Bridging American Bourbon to the World

result is water that is not only ideal for making bourbon but also incredibly fresh and healthful.

For Di Tran, the Ohio River is a symbol of Kentucky's natural bounty—a reminder that the land itself is a gift, providing everything needed to create something as extraordinary as bourbon. The water that flows through the river, the limestone that filters it, and the rich soil that grows the corn all come together to create the perfect environment for bourbon production. It is a harmony of natural elements that is as beautiful as it is powerful.

The Limestone Foundation: The Secret Ingredient

Kentucky's limestone foundation is often referred to as the secret ingredient in the state's bourbon. This limestone, formed millions of years ago from the skeletal remains of ancient sea creatures, is abundant throughout the state, particularly in the central Bluegrass region. It is this limestone that gives Kentucky its fertile soil, its rich water, and, ultimately, its world-renowned bourbon.

The limestone not only filters the water but also contributes to the state's agricultural success, providing the ideal conditions for growing the corn that is essential to bourbon production. The calcium-rich soil, combined with the state's climate, produces

Kentucky Bourbon: The Pride of the Bluegrass State
Di Tran Bourbon BELIEF: Bridging American Bourbon to the World

corn that is sweet, flavorful, and perfect for making bourbon.

For Di Tran, the limestone foundation of Kentucky is a metaphor for the strength and resilience of the people who live there. Just as the limestone provides a solid foundation for the state's natural resources, so too does it provide a foundation for the culture of Kentucky—a culture that is rooted in tradition, yet open to innovation; that values community, yet celebrates individuality.

The People of Kentucky: Strength in Diversity

Kentucky is a state of contrasts—urban and rural, traditional and modern, diverse and unified. It is a place where people from all walks of life come together to create a community that is as strong and resilient as the limestone beneath their feet. The people of Kentucky are known for their warmth, their hospitality, and their unwavering belief in the importance of community.

For Di Tran, who came to Kentucky as an immigrant from Vietnam, this sense of community was one of the first things he noticed—and one of the things he has come to cherish the most. In Kentucky, he found a place where people welcomed him with open arms, where they were eager to share their culture and

Kentucky Bourbon: The Pride of the Bluegrass State
Di Tran Bourbon BELIEF: Bridging American Bourbon to the World

traditions, and where they were genuinely interested in learning about his.

This spirit of inclusiveness and hospitality is at the heart of Kentucky's culture. It is a place where people are strong, not just in the sense of physical or emotional strength, but in the sense of being grounded, confident, and secure in who they are. This strength is reflected in the way they live their lives, in the way they treat others, and in the way they come together to support one another.

Kentucky's culture is one of connection—connection to the land, to the seasons, to the community, and to the traditions that have been passed down through generations. This is the culture that Di Tran Bourbon BELIEF seeks to embody—a culture of warmth, hospitality, and an unwavering belief in the power of human connection.

Bourbon as a Celebration of Life

In Kentucky, drinking bourbon is about more than just enjoying a good drink; it is about celebrating life. It is about taking the time to savor the moment, to reflect on the things that matter most, and to connect with the people around you. Whether it's a quiet evening at home, a gathering with friends, or a special occasion,

Kentucky Bourbon: The Pride of the Bluegrass State
Di Tran Bourbon BELIEF: Bridging American Bourbon to the World

bourbon is a way to mark the moment, to acknowledge the beauty of life, and to share that beauty with others.

Di Tran Bourbon BELIEF embodies this ethos of celebration. It is a bourbon that is meant to be shared, to bring people together, and to create moments of connection and meaning. It is a bourbon that encourages reflection, relaxation, and meaningful dialogue—a drink for those who seek to elevate each other, to foster a sense of togetherness, and to build a better future, one conversation at a time.

For Di Tran, bourbon is not just a drink; it is a symbol of everything that makes Kentucky special. It is a reflection of the state's natural beauty, its rich history, and its vibrant culture. It is a way to connect with the land, with the people, and with the traditions that have shaped Kentucky into the place it is today.

The Seasons of Bourbon: A Year in the Life

In Kentucky, the changing seasons are a reminder of the passage of time, of the cycles of life, and of the beauty that comes with each new season. This is particularly true in the world of bourbon, where the seasons play a crucial role in the aging process, shaping the character and flavor of the spirit.

Kentucky Bourbon: The Pride of the Bluegrass State
Di Tran Bourbon BELIEF: Bridging American Bourbon to the World

Spring is a time of renewal, a time when the bourbon begins to awaken from its winter slumber, absorbing the fresh air and the new life that comes with the season. The barrels, which have contracted during the cold winter months, begin to expand, allowing the bourbon to interact more fully with the wood, drawing out the rich flavors of caramel, vanilla, and spice.

Summer is a time of growth, a time when the heat causes the bourbon to expand even further, pushing deeper into the wood and absorbing the flavors that will define its character. The warm, humid air of Kentucky's summer accelerates the aging process, bringing out the sweetness of the corn and the richness of the oak.

Autumn is a time of harvest, a time when the bourbon begins to mature, developing the complexity and depth that comes with time. The cooler temperatures slow the aging process, allowing the flavors to meld and harmonize, creating a spirit that is rich, smooth, and full-bodied.

Winter is a time of rest, a time when the bourbon slows its aging process, allowing the spirit to mellow and refine. The cold air causes the barrels to contract, drawing the bourbon back into the center, where it rests, absorbing the last of the flavors from the wood,

Kentucky Bourbon: The Pride of the Bluegrass State
Di Tran Bourbon BELIEF: Bridging American Bourbon to the World

and developing the smooth finish that is the hallmark of a well-aged bourbon.

For Di Tran, the seasons of bourbon are a reflection of the seasons of life. Each season brings its own challenges and rewards, its own beauty and complexity. Just as the bourbon is shaped by the seasons, so too are we shaped by the experiences we go through, the challenges we face, and the people we meet along the way.

Building a Better Future: One Conversation at a Time

In Kentucky, there is a deep belief in the power of conversation, in the idea that the best way to build a better future is by coming together, sharing ideas, and working towards a common goal. This belief is reflected in the way people live their lives, in the way they treat each other, and in the way they approach the challenges and opportunities that come their way.

Di Tran Bourbon BELIEF is a bourbon that is designed to facilitate these conversations. It is a bourbon that encourages people to sit down, to take the time to listen to each other, and to find common ground. It is a bourbon that fosters a sense of community, that brings people together, and that helps to build the connections that are necessary for creating a better future.

Kentucky Bourbon: The Pride of the Bluegrass State
Di Tran Bourbon BELIEF: Bridging American Bourbon to the World

For Di Tran, this is the true essence of Kentucky's culture—a culture of warmth, hospitality, and an unwavering belief in the power of human connection. It is a culture that is reflected in every bottle of Di Tran Bourbon BELIEF, a culture that celebrates life, that values community, and that believes in the importance of building a better future, one conversation at a time.

Conclusion: The Tapestry of Kentucky

Kentucky is a state that is rich in history, in culture, and in natural beauty. It is a place where the seasons change with a rhythm that is as predictable as it is beautiful, where the land provides everything needed to create something as extraordinary as bourbon, and where the people are as strong and resilient as the limestone beneath their feet.

Di Tran Bourbon BELIEF is a reflection of this cultural tapestry—a bourbon that embodies the warmth, the hospitality, and the sense of community that make Kentucky so special. It is a bourbon that celebrates life, that encourages meaningful conversation, and that helps to build the connections that are necessary for creating a better future.

As you sip Di Tran Bourbon BELIEF, you are not just enjoying a fine bourbon; you are participating in a tradition that has been passed down through

Kentucky Bourbon: The Pride of the Bluegrass State
Di Tran Bourbon BELIEF: Bridging American Bourbon to the World

generations, a tradition that is rooted in the land, in the seasons, and in the people of Kentucky. It is a tradition that values authenticity, that celebrates the beauty of the world around us, and that believes in the power of human connection.

This is the cultural tapestry of Kentucky—a tapestry that is as rich and vibrant as the bourbon it produces, and one that will continue to inspire and connect people for generations to come.

Chapter 5: Bourbon vs. The World

Kentucky Bourbon: A Global Contender

In the vast and diverse world of spirits, Kentucky bourbon has carved out a niche that is both distinctive and revered. While the world boasts a plethora of exceptional spirits—from the refined sophistication of French Cognac to the storied heritage of Irish whiskey and the crisp clarity of vodka—Kentucky bourbon stands out as a unique offering that combines sweetness, spice, and strength in a way that few other spirits can match. It is a spirit deeply rooted in its Kentucky origins, yet it has a global appeal that transcends borders and cultures.

Kentucky Bourbon: The Pride of the Bluegrass State
Di Tran Bourbon BELIEF: Bridging American Bourbon to the World

The rise of bourbon on the international stage is no accident. It is the result of centuries of craftsmanship, a unique climate that perfectly suits the aging process, and a culture that values authenticity and quality above all else. Di Tran Bourbon BELIEF is a shining example of this tradition, offering a rich, full-bodied flavor that showcases the best of what Kentucky bourbon has to offer. As bourbon continues to gain popularity worldwide, it is clear that this uniquely American spirit is poised to become a dominant force in the global liquor industry over the next decade.

The Unique Appeal of Kentucky Bourbon

To understand why Kentucky bourbon has captured the hearts and palates of drinkers around the world, it is important to examine what sets it apart from other spirits. At its core, bourbon is defined by its primary ingredient—corn, which must make up at least 51% of the mash bill. This gives bourbon its characteristic sweetness, a quality that distinguishes it from other whiskies, which often have a more pronounced malt or rye flavor.

But bourbon is more than just sweet. The aging process in new charred oak barrels imparts a depth of flavor that includes notes of caramel, vanilla, and spice. These flavors are enhanced by the unique

Kentucky Bourbon: The Pride of the Bluegrass State
Di Tran Bourbon BELIEF: Bridging American Bourbon to the World

climate of Kentucky, where the hot summers and cold winters cause the bourbon to expand and contract within the barrels, drawing out the rich flavors of the wood. The result is a spirit that is smooth, yet complex; sweet, yet bold; a perfect balance of flavors that appeals to both seasoned connoisseurs and newcomers alike.

Di Tran Bourbon BELIEF embodies these qualities to perfection. Aged for eight years, it offers a rich, full-bodied flavor that is both smooth and powerful. The high proof of the bourbon delivers a kick that is tempered by its smooth finish, making it a drink that can be enjoyed neat, on the rocks, or as the base of a sophisticated cocktail. It is a bourbon that stays true to its Kentucky roots, yet it is sophisticated enough to hold its own against the finest spirits from around the world.

Bourbon vs. Cognac: The Battle of Sophistication

Cognac, a brandy from the Cognac region of France, has long been associated with sophistication and luxury. It is a spirit that is often enjoyed after dinner, sipped slowly in a snifter, and appreciated for its complex flavors and aromas. Like bourbon, Cognac is aged in oak barrels, which gives it a rich, amber color and imparts flavors of vanilla, caramel, and spice.

Kentucky Bourbon: The Pride of the Bluegrass State
Di Tran Bourbon BELIEF: Bridging American Bourbon to the World

However, there are key differences between the two spirits that give bourbon a unique edge. While Cognac is made from grapes, bourbon is made from corn, giving it a natural sweetness that Cognac lacks. This sweetness is balanced by the bold flavors imparted by the charred oak barrels, creating a spirit that is both complex and approachable. Bourbon also has a higher alcohol content than Cognac, which gives it a stronger kick and a more pronounced flavor profile.

Di Tran Bourbon BELIEF, with its full-bodied flavor and high proof, exemplifies the qualities that set bourbon apart from Cognac. It is a spirit that can be enjoyed in the same sophisticated settings as Cognac, yet it offers a bolder, more robust experience. The smooth finish of the bourbon, coupled with its powerful kick, makes it a drink that is both refined and exciting—a perfect choice for those who appreciate the finer things in life, but who also crave a spirit with a bit more punch.

Bourbon vs. Irish Whiskey: A Tale of Heritage

Irish whiskey is another spirit with a long and storied history. Known for its smooth, mellow flavor, Irish whiskey is often triple-distilled, which gives it a light, clean taste that is easy to drink. It is a spirit that is

Kentucky Bourbon: The Pride of the Bluegrass State
Di Tran Bourbon BELIEF: Bridging American Bourbon to the World

deeply connected to Irish culture and tradition, and it is enjoyed by millions of people around the world.

However, while Irish whiskey is known for its smoothness, it often lacks the depth and complexity that bourbon offers. The use of corn in bourbon's mash bill, along with the aging process in new charred oak barrels, gives bourbon a richer, more robust flavor profile. Bourbon also has a higher alcohol content than most Irish whiskies, which gives it a stronger presence on the palate.

Di Tran Bourbon BELIEF takes these qualities to the next level. Its rich, full-bodied flavor is complemented by a smooth finish that rivals the best Irish whiskies, yet it has a depth and complexity that sets it apart. The aging process, coupled with the high proof of the bourbon, creates a spirit that is both powerful and refined—a drink that pays homage to the heritage of Kentucky while offering a unique experience that can stand toe-to-toe with the finest Irish whiskies.

Bourbon vs. Rum: The Battle of Sweetness

Rum, particularly dark or aged rum, shares some similarities with bourbon in terms of flavor profile. Both spirits are known for their sweetness, which comes from the use of sugarcane in rum and corn in

Kentucky Bourbon: The Pride of the Bluegrass State
Di Tran Bourbon BELIEF: Bridging American Bourbon to the World

bourbon. Both are also aged in oak barrels, which imparts rich flavors of caramel, vanilla, and spice.

However, while rum is often associated with tropical flavors and cocktails, bourbon is known for its versatility and its ability to stand alone as a sipping spirit. The complexity of bourbon, with its combination of sweetness, spice, and strength, makes it a more sophisticated choice for those who appreciate a spirit that offers more than just sweetness.

Di Tran Bourbon BELIEF exemplifies this sophistication. Its rich, full-bodied flavor is complemented by a smooth finish that makes it a perfect choice for sipping neat or on the rocks. The high proof of the bourbon adds an extra layer of complexity, making it a spirit that can be enjoyed in a variety of settings, from a casual evening at home to a formal celebration. While rum may be the go-to choice for tropical cocktails, bourbon, particularly Di Tran Bourbon BELIEF, is the spirit of choice for those who appreciate a more refined and complex drinking experience.

Bourbon vs. Vodka: The Clash of Clear and Dark

Vodka, with its neutral flavor profile and clear appearance, is one of the most versatile spirits in the world. It is often used as a base for cocktails, where its

Kentucky Bourbon: The Pride of the Bluegrass State
Di Tran Bourbon BELIEF: Bridging American Bourbon to the World

lack of strong flavor allows other ingredients to shine. Vodka is also known for its smoothness, which makes it easy to drink, but it often lacks the complexity and depth that bourbon offers.

Bourbon, on the other hand, is a spirit that is rich in flavor and character. Its amber color and full-bodied flavor are the result of years spent aging in charred oak barrels, a process that imparts a complexity that vodka simply cannot match. While vodka may be the spirit of choice for those who prefer a light, easy-to-drink cocktail, bourbon is the go-to choice for those who appreciate a spirit with depth and character.

Di Tran Bourbon BELIEF stands as a testament to the complexity and depth that bourbon offers. Its rich, full-bodied flavor is complemented by a smooth finish, making it a perfect choice for those who appreciate a spirit that offers more than just a neutral base for cocktails. Whether enjoyed neat, on the rocks, or as the base of a sophisticated cocktail, Di Tran Bourbon BELIEF offers a drinking experience that is unmatched by vodka.

Di Tran Bourbon BELIEF: A Spirit That Transcends Borders

While Kentucky bourbon is deeply rooted in its American origins, it is a spirit that has the power to

Kentucky Bourbon: The Pride of the Bluegrass State
Di Tran Bourbon BELIEF: Bridging American Bourbon to the World

transcend borders and cultures. Di Tran Bourbon BELIEF, with its rich, full-bodied flavor and smooth finish, is a perfect example of this global appeal. Crafted in the heart of Kentucky, yet sophisticated enough to be enjoyed by drinkers around the world, it is a bourbon that is poised to make a significant impact on the global liquor industry.

The potential for bourbon to dominate the global market is evident in the increasing demand for premium spirits, particularly in emerging markets like Asia. Vietnam, with its rapidly growing middle class and increasing interest in Western luxury goods, represents a significant opportunity for bourbon producers. Di Tran, with his deep connections to both Kentucky and Vietnam, is uniquely positioned to take advantage of this opportunity, using Louisville's strategic location as a hub for global distribution.

Louisville: The Gateway to the World

Louisville, Kentucky, home to UPS's global headquarters, is a city that is perfectly positioned to serve as a gateway for bourbon to the world. With its central location and world-class logistics infrastructure, Louisville is a natural hub for the distribution of bourbon to markets around the globe. This makes it an ideal base for Di Tran Bourbon

Kentucky Bourbon: The Pride of the Bluegrass State
Di Tran Bourbon BELIEF: Bridging American Bourbon to the World

BELIEF as it expands its reach beyond the United States.

The partnership between Di Tran Bourbon BELIEF and UPS represents a strategic alliance that can help propel bourbon to new heights on the global stage. By leveraging Louisville's logistics capabilities and Di Tran's unique understanding of both American and Asian markets, Di Tran Bourbon BELIEF is poised to become a major player in the global spirits industry.

Vietnam: The Anchor for Bourbon in Asia

Vietnam, with its growing economy and increasing interest in premium spirits, represents a key market for bourbon's global expansion. As an anchor for bourbon distribution in Asia, Vietnam offers a unique opportunity for Di Tran Bourbon BELIEF to establish itself as a leading brand in the region. The country's young, dynamic population is increasingly interested in Western luxury goods, and bourbon, with its rich history and sophisticated flavor profile, is a perfect fit for this market.

Di Tran's deep connections to Vietnam, combined with his understanding of both Kentucky and Vietnamese cultures, give him a unique advantage in this market. By introducing Di Tran Bourbon BELIEF to Vietnam, he is not just bringing a new product to the

Kentucky Bourbon: The Pride of the Bluegrass State
Di Tran Bourbon BELIEF: Bridging American Bourbon to the World

market; he is sharing a piece of Kentucky's rich heritage with a new audience, creating a bridge between two cultures that are both deeply rooted in tradition and craftsmanship.

Bourbon's Global Future: A Dominant Force in the Next Decade

As the global demand for premium spirits continues to grow, bourbon is well-positioned to become a dominant force in the liquor industry over the next decade. The unique combination of sweetness, spice, and strength that bourbon offers, coupled with its rich history and deep cultural roots, makes it a spirit that resonates with drinkers around the world.

Di Tran Bourbon BELIEF, with its rich, full-bodied flavor and smooth finish, exemplifies the qualities that make bourbon so special. As it expands its reach into new markets, particularly in Asia, it has the potential to become a leading brand in the global spirits industry. The strategic partnership with UPS and the focus on key markets like Vietnam position Di Tran Bourbon BELIEF to be at the forefront of bourbon's global expansion.

In the next five to ten years, bourbon is poised to take over the world, becoming a go-to spirit for those who appreciate quality, craftsmanship, and a rich, complex

Kentucky Bourbon: The Pride of the Bluegrass State
Di Tran Bourbon BELIEF: Bridging American Bourbon to the World

flavor profile. Di Tran Bourbon BELIEF is leading the charge, offering a bourbon that is both deeply rooted in its Kentucky origins and sophisticated enough to appeal to drinkers around the world. As bourbon continues to grow in popularity, it is clear that this uniquely American spirit is ready to take its place on the global stage, bringing the best of Kentucky to the world.

Kentucky Bourbon: The Pride of the Bluegrass State
Di Tran Bourbon BELIEF: Bridging American Bourbon to the World

Chapter 6: The Craft of Belief – Creating Di Tran Bourbon

The Art of Crafting Bourbon: A Tradition of Excellence

Crafting Di Tran Bourbon BELIEF is not just a process; it is an art form, steeped in tradition and driven by a deep-seated belief in quality. Every bottle of Di Tran Bourbon BELIEF represents a commitment to excellence, a dedication to the craft that has defined Kentucky bourbon for centuries. From the selection of the finest grains to the careful aging in charred oak barrels, each step is executed with precision and care, ensuring that the final product is nothing short of extraordinary.

Bourbon, by its very nature, is a spirit that requires patience, skill, and an unwavering commitment to quality. The journey of Di Tran Bourbon BELIEF begins with the careful selection of ingredients, sourced from the rich farmlands of Kentucky. It continues through the meticulous process of distillation and aging, where time and tradition work hand in hand to create a spirit that is both complex and refined. But what sets Di Tran Bourbon BELIEF apart is not just the process, but the belief that drives it—a belief in the

Kentucky Bourbon: The Pride of the Bluegrass State
Di Tran Bourbon BELIEF: Bridging American Bourbon to the World

power of authenticity, in the importance of tradition, and in the value of creating something truly special.

Sourcing from the Best: A Partnership with Kentucky's Finest

The journey of Di Tran Bourbon BELIEF starts with its source—a partnership with one of Kentucky's top 10 distilleries, known for its expertise and long-standing tradition in bourbon making. This distillery, with its deep-rooted history and commitment to excellence, provides the foundation for what makes Di Tran Bourbon BELIEF so unique. The distillery's decades of experience in crafting world-class bourbon ensure that only the finest spirits are selected for aging.

The decision to source from this particular distillery was not made lightly. Di Tran recognized that to create a bourbon that truly stands out, he needed to start with the best. This distillery, with its reputation for producing some of the finest bourbons in the world, was the perfect partner. The bourbon selected for Di Tran Bourbon BELIEF is aged for eight years—longer than many bourbons on the market—allowing it to develop a richness and depth of flavor that is unparalleled.

The Magic of Aging: Eight Years of Perfection

Kentucky Bourbon: The Pride of the Bluegrass State
Di Tran Bourbon BELIEF: Bridging American Bourbon to the World

Aging is where the magic happens in bourbon making, and for Di Tran Bourbon BELIEF, this process is particularly special. The bourbon is aged for a full eight years in new charred oak barrels, a process that allows it to absorb the rich flavors of the wood and develop the complex, full-bodied profile that sets it apart. During these eight years, the bourbon is exposed to Kentucky's unique climate, where hot summers and cold winters cause the spirit to expand and contract within the barrels. This interaction with the wood imparts deep flavors of caramel, vanilla, and spice, along with the smoothness and balance that only time can bring.

Most bourbons on the market today are aged for a shorter period, but Di Tran Bourbon BELIEF is aged longer to achieve a level of complexity and refinement that is truly exceptional. The decision to age the bourbon for eight years was a deliberate one, based on the belief that time is an essential ingredient in creating a spirit of this caliber. The result is a bourbon that is rich, smooth, and full of character—a spirit that can be savored on its own or shared with others in moments of connection and celebration.

Straight from the Barrel: A Unique Offering

Kentucky Bourbon: The Pride of the Bluegrass State
Di Tran Bourbon BELIEF: Bridging American Bourbon to the World

One of the most distinctive features of Di Tran Bourbon BELIEF is that it is bottled straight from the barrel, without dilution. This means that what you taste in the bottle is exactly what was in the barrel—nothing added, nothing taken away. This approach is rare in the bourbon world, where many spirits are diluted before bottling to achieve a lower proof. By bottling straight from the barrel, Di Tran Bourbon BELIEF offers a pure, unadulterated bourbon experience that is both powerful and authentic.

This decision to bottle straight from the barrel is a reflection of Di Tran's commitment to authenticity. He believes that the best things in life should be experienced in their purest form, and this philosophy is evident in every sip of Di Tran Bourbon BELIEF. The high proof of the bourbon—often over 120 proof—delivers a bold, intense flavor that is balanced by the smoothness that comes from years of aging. It is a bourbon that commands attention, a spirit that is meant to be savored and appreciated.

The Craftsmanship Behind Di Tran Bourbon BELIEF

Crafting Di Tran Bourbon BELIEF is a labor of love, a process that involves not just skill, but passion and dedication. Every step of the process, from selecting

Kentucky Bourbon: The Pride of the Bluegrass State
Di Tran Bourbon BELIEF: Bridging American Bourbon to the World

the grains to bottling the final product, is carried out with meticulous care. The grains used in the bourbon are sourced from Kentucky's finest farms, where the soil and climate produce some of the best corn, rye, and barley in the world. These grains are carefully milled, mashed, and fermented, creating a mash that is rich in flavor and perfect for distillation.

The distillation process itself is a delicate art, one that requires precise control and expert knowledge. The mash is distilled in copper stills, where it is heated and condensed to create a spirit that is both clean and flavorful. The distillers at the partnering distillery use their years of experience to ensure that only the finest cuts of the distillate make it into the barrels for aging. This attention to detail is what sets Di Tran Bourbon BELIEF apart, ensuring that every bottle is of the highest quality.

The barrels used for aging are another critical component of the process. Made from American white oak, these barrels are charred on the inside to create a layer of caramelized wood sugars that interact with the bourbon during aging. The barrels are carefully selected and monitored throughout the aging process to ensure that they impart the perfect balance of flavor and complexity. The result is a bourbon that is rich, smooth, and full of character—a spirit that truly embodies the art of bourbon making.

A Limited Edition with Unmatched Quality

Di Tran Bourbon BELIEF is not just any bourbon; it is a limited edition release, crafted with the utmost care and attention to detail. Each bottle is part of a small batch, ensuring that every aspect of the bourbon, from the selection of the grains to the aging process, is carefully controlled and monitored. This limited edition release is a testament to the dedication and passion that goes into creating Di Tran Bourbon BELIEF, making it a truly special and rare offering in the world of bourbon.

The decision to release Di Tran Bourbon BELIEF as a limited edition was driven by a desire to create something truly unique—something that stands out in a crowded market and offers a bourbon experience unlike any other. By limiting the number of bottles produced, Di Tran ensures that each bottle receives the attention and care it deserves, resulting in a product of unmatched quality. This commitment to quality is what makes Di Tran Bourbon BELIEF so special, and why it has quickly become a sought-after item among bourbon enthusiasts.

Kentucky Bourbon: The Pride of the Bluegrass State
Di Tran Bourbon BELIEF: Bridging American Bourbon to the World

The Future of Di Tran Bourbon: A Commitment to Innovation and Tradition

While Di Tran Bourbon BELIEF is a limited edition release, it is just the beginning of what Di Tran has planned for the future. Building on the success of this initial release, Di Tran is committed to continuing to push the boundaries of what bourbon can be, while staying true to the traditions that have made Kentucky bourbon so revered. Future releases from Di Tran Bourbon will feature multiple unique offerings, each crafted with the same dedication to quality and tradition that defines Di Tran Bourbon BELIEF.

These future releases will continue to showcase the art of bourbon making, with high-proof, barrel-strength offerings that reflect Di Tran's commitment to authenticity and excellence. Each release will be carefully crafted to highlight the unique qualities of Kentucky bourbon, while also offering something new and exciting for bourbon enthusiasts. Whether it's a new aging process, a different mash bill, or a unique finish, Di Tran is committed to innovation, always seeking to create something truly special.

But no matter how innovative these future releases may be, they will always be rooted in the traditions of Kentucky bourbon, and in the belief that quality and

Kentucky Bourbon: The Pride of the Bluegrass State
Di Tran Bourbon BELIEF: Bridging American Bourbon to the World

craftsmanship are the cornerstones of any great spirit. This commitment to tradition and innovation is what makes Di Tran Bourbon so special, and why it will continue to be a leader in the bourbon industry for years to come.

Pride in Heritage: Vietnamese Origin, American Craftsmanship

Di Tran Bourbon BELIEF is more than just a bourbon; it is a reflection of Di Tran's journey and heritage. Born in Vietnam and now proudly American, Di Tran brings a unique perspective to the world of bourbon making. His heritage is a source of pride, and it influences everything he does, from the way he approaches the craft of bourbon making to the way he connects with others.

Di Tran's journey from Vietnam to America is one of perseverance, dedication, and a deep belief in the power of hard work. These values are reflected in every bottle of Di Tran Bourbon BELIEF, a bourbon that embodies the best of both worlds—the rich traditions of Kentucky bourbon and the strength and resilience of the Vietnamese spirit. Di Tran Bourbon BELIEF is a celebration of this heritage, and of the opportunities that America has provided.

Kentucky Bourbon: The Pride of the Bluegrass State
Di Tran Bourbon BELIEF: Bridging American Bourbon to the World

This pride in heritage is also reflected in Di Tran's commitment to his adopted home of Louisville, Kentucky. As a Louisvillian and a proud citizen of Kentucky, Di Tran is dedicated to contributing to the rich cultural tapestry of the state and to sharing the best of Kentucky bourbon with the world. Di Tran Bourbon BELIEF is a testament to this commitment, and to the belief that great things can be achieved when tradition and innovation come together.

Conclusion: The Art of Belief

Crafting Di Tran Bourbon BELIEF is an art, one that requires skill, dedication, and a deep belief in quality and tradition. From the careful selection of the finest grains to the meticulous aging process, every step is a testament to the craftsmanship that defines Kentucky bourbon. But more than that, it is a reflection of the belief that drives Di Tran—belief in the power of authenticity, in the importance of tradition, and in the value of creating something truly special.

Di Tran Bourbon BELIEF is a bourbon that stands out in a crowded market, offering a unique experience that is both powerful and refined. It is a spirit that is rooted in the traditions of Kentucky bourbon, yet innovative enough to appeal to a new generation of bourbon enthusiasts. As Di Tran continues to push the

Kentucky Bourbon: The Pride of the Bluegrass State
Di Tran Bourbon BELIEF: Bridging American Bourbon to the World

boundaries of what bourbon can be, while staying true to the traditions that have made Kentucky bourbon so revered, there is no doubt that Di Tran Bourbon BELIEF will continue to be a leader in the industry.

This is the art of belief—the belief that quality, tradition, and innovation can come together to create something truly extraordinary. And it is this belief that will continue to guide Di Tran Bourbon as it grows and evolves, always striving to create the best bourbon possible, and to share that bourbon with the world.

Kentucky Bourbon: The Pride of the Bluegrass State
Di Tran Bourbon BELIEF: Bridging American Bourbon to the World

Chapter 7: A Toast to Humanity

The Essence of Celebration

In the hustle and bustle of modern life, it's easy to forget the importance of celebration. Not the kind of celebration marked by grand gestures or excessive indulgence, but the quiet, meaningful moments that remind us of the beauty of existence. Di Tran Bourbon BELIEF is crafted for these moments—a drink designed not to intoxicate but to elevate, to bring people together, and to create connections that transcend the ordinary. This bourbon is more than just a spirit; it's a symbol of unity, a testament to the belief that we are better when we are united in appreciation of life's simple, yet profound, joys.

From the moment the bottle is opened, Di Tran Bourbon BELIEF invites you to slow down, to savor the moment, and to connect with those around you. It's a drink that fosters conversation, that deepens relationships, and that helps you see the world in a different light. Whether it's a quiet evening after a long day or a gathering of loved ones, Di Tran Bourbon BELIEF is there to enhance the experience, to make it more memorable, more meaningful.

Beyond a Drink: A Spiritual Experience

Kentucky Bourbon: The Pride of the Bluegrass State
Di Tran Bourbon BELIEF: Bridging American Bourbon to the World

Drinking Di Tran Bourbon BELIEF is not just about enjoying a finely crafted bourbon; it's about embarking on a journey—a spiritual journey that takes you beyond the physical world and into the realms of the soul, the divine, and the universe. There's something almost mystical about the experience of sipping this bourbon, something that transcends the ordinary and touches the extraordinary. It's as if each sip opens a door to a deeper understanding of yourself, of those around you, and of the world you inhabit.

In many ways, Di Tran Bourbon BELIEF is akin to a spiritual ritual, one that allows you to connect with a higher state of consciousness. Just as meditation can bring you to a place of inner peace and clarity, so too can this bourbon guide you to a state where you can appreciate the beauty of life, the connections between people, and the presence of something greater than yourself. It's a drink that doesn't just warm the body but also nourishes the soul, helping you to see beyond the material and into the spiritual.

The Theta and Alpha State: Connecting with the Divine

There are moments in life when we transcend our usual state of consciousness—moments when we enter a state of flow, of peace, of connection with something

Kentucky Bourbon: The Pride of the Bluegrass State
Di Tran Bourbon BELIEF: Bridging American Bourbon to the World

greater. In the world of neuroscience, these states are often associated with theta and alpha brainwaves, the frequencies that are linked to relaxation, creativity, and deep meditation. Di Tran Bourbon BELIEF is a catalyst for reaching these states, a drink that gently guides you into a place of calm and clarity, where the boundaries between yourself and the universe begin to blur.

As you sip Di Tran Bourbon BELIEF, you might find yourself slipping into a meditative state, where the worries of the day fall away, and all that remains is a sense of oneness with the world. It's in these moments that you can truly appreciate the beauty of life—the gentle warmth of the bourbon as it travels down your throat, the rich flavors that dance on your palate, and the feeling of connection with those around you. This is the power of Di Tran Bourbon BELIEF—it's not just a drink, but a tool for reaching a state of consciousness where you can connect with your soul, with God, and with the universe.

The Beauty of Life: A Divine Appreciation

There's a profound beauty in life that often goes unnoticed in the rush of daily living. It's the beauty of a sunset, the sound of laughter, the feel of a loved one's hand in yours. Di Tran Bourbon BELIEF is a

Kentucky Bourbon: The Pride of the Bluegrass State
Di Tran Bourbon BELIEF: Bridging American Bourbon to the World

celebration of this beauty—a drink that encourages you to slow down, to look around, and to appreciate the world in all its glory. It's a reminder that life is not just about doing, but about being—about existing in the moment and finding joy in the simple things.

In this way, Di Tran Bourbon BELIEF is a testament to the beauty of God, the creator of all that is beautiful and good in the world. Each sip is a reminder of the divine, a way to connect with the spiritual essence that flows through all things. Whether you're sitting alone in quiet reflection or surrounded by friends and family, Di Tran Bourbon BELIEF helps you to see the world through new eyes, to find the sacred in the ordinary, and to celebrate the gift of life.

A Drink That Binds Us Together

In a world that often feels divided, where differences are highlighted more than commonalities, Di Tran Bourbon BELIEF is a drink that brings people together. It's a unifying force, a way to bridge the gaps between us and to foster a sense of community and connection. There's something about sharing a glass of bourbon that breaks down barriers, that encourages openness and honesty, and that reminds us of our shared humanity.

Kentucky Bourbon: The Pride of the Bluegrass State
Di Tran Bourbon BELIEF: Bridging American Bourbon to the World

When you pour a glass of Di Tran Bourbon BELIEF, you're not just pouring a drink; you're pouring an opportunity for connection. It's a way to engage in meaningful conversation, to share stories and experiences, and to create bonds that go beyond the superficial. This is the essence of Di Tran Bourbon BELIEF—a belief in the power of connection, in the idea that we are stronger, better, and happier when we are united in celebration of life's moments, big and small.

The Role of Ritual: Creating Sacred Moments

Rituals have always played a significant role in human culture, serving as a way to mark important moments, to connect with the divine, and to bring people together. Drinking Di Tran Bourbon BELIEF is, in many ways, a modern ritual—a way to create sacred moments in the midst of everyday life. It's about taking the time to slow down, to be present, and to engage fully with the experience of drinking a finely crafted bourbon.

This ritual begins the moment you open the bottle, releasing the rich aromas that have been locked inside during the aging process. As you pour the bourbon into a glass, you're engaging in a time-honored tradition, one that has been passed down through generations.

Kentucky Bourbon: The Pride of the Bluegrass State
Di Tran Bourbon BELIEF: Bridging American Bourbon to the World

And as you raise the glass to your lips, you're participating in a ritual that is about more than just drinking—it's about celebrating life, honoring the connections between people, and recognizing the beauty of the world around you.

The Healing Power of Connection

In a world where so many people feel disconnected—disconnected from themselves, from others, and from the world—Di Tran Bourbon BELIEF offers a way to reconnect. It's a drink that encourages you to be present, to engage with those around you, and to find healing in the simple act of sharing a glass of bourbon. There's something profoundly healing about being with others, about sharing stories and experiences, and about finding common ground over a shared drink.

Di Tran Bourbon BELIEF is designed for these moments of connection. It's a drink that doesn't just satisfy the senses, but that also nourishes the soul. Whether you're catching up with an old friend, celebrating a special occasion, or simply unwinding after a long day, Di Tran Bourbon BELIEF helps you to reconnect—with yourself, with others, and with the world. It's a reminder that, in the end, what matters most are the connections we make, the relationships we build, and the moments we share.

Kentucky Bourbon: The Pride of the Bluegrass State
Di Tran Bourbon BELIEF: Bridging American Bourbon to the World

The Universality of Celebration

One of the most beautiful aspects of Di Tran Bourbon BELIEF is its universality. It's a drink that transcends cultural and geographic boundaries, one that can be enjoyed by people from all walks of life. Whether you're in Kentucky, Vietnam, or anywhere in between, Di Tran Bourbon BELIEF is a drink that brings people together, fostering a sense of unity and shared experience.

In this way, Di Tran Bourbon BELIEF is more than just a bourbon; it's a celebration of humanity. It's a recognition of the fact that, no matter where we come from or what our backgrounds are, we all share the same basic desires—to connect, to celebrate, and to find meaning in the moments that make up our lives. By bringing people together over a shared drink, Di Tran Bourbon BELIEF helps to create a sense of global community, one that is rooted in the belief that we are all part of something greater.

A Toast to Life's Moments

There are certain moments in life that deserve to be celebrated—moments of joy, of achievement, of connection. These are the moments that define us, that give our lives meaning, and that remind us of the beauty of existence. Di Tran Bourbon BELIEF is crafted for these moments, a drink that is meant to be raised in a toast to life's most meaningful experiences.

Whether it's a wedding, a graduation, a reunion, or simply a quiet evening at home, Di Tran Bourbon BELIEF adds something special to the occasion. It's a drink that elevates the moment, that makes it more memorable, more meaningful. And as you raise your glass, you're not just toasting the occasion—you're toasting life itself, with all its joys, challenges, and beauty.

The Legacy of Di Tran Bourbon BELIEF

As you sip Di Tran Bourbon BELIEF, you're not just enjoying a finely crafted bourbon; you're participating in a legacy. This bourbon is the result of years of dedication, of a commitment to quality, and of a belief in the power of connection. It's a legacy that is rooted in tradition, yet one that looks forward to the future, to the new connections, new celebrations, and new moments that will be made with each bottle.

This legacy is about more than just making a great bourbon; it's about making a difference. It's about creating something that brings people together, that fosters connection, and that adds meaning to life's moments. And it's about passing this legacy on to future generations, ensuring that the values of connection, celebration, and appreciation of life's beauty continue to thrive.

Conclusion: A Spiritual Toast

In the end, Di Tran Bourbon BELIEF is more than just a drink; it's a spiritual experience, a way to connect with the divine, with others, and with the beauty of the world. It's a reminder that life is not just about surviving, but about thriving—about finding joy, meaning, and connection in the moments that make up our lives. Whether you're raising a glass to celebrate a special occasion or simply enjoying a quiet moment of reflection, Di Tran Bourbon BELIEF is there to enhance the experience, to make it more meaningful, more spiritual.

So here's to life, to connection, to the beauty of existence, and to the belief that we are all part of something greater. Here's to the moments that define us, the people who inspire us, and the spirit that brings us together. Here's to Di Tran Bourbon BELIEF—a toast to humanity, and to the belief that we are better when we are united in celebration of life's most meaningful moments.

Kentucky Bourbon: The Pride of the Bluegrass State
Di Tran Bourbon BELIEF: Bridging American Bourbon to the World

Chapter 8: Beyond the Bottle – The Legacy of Di Tran Bourbon

A Legacy in the Making

When Di Tran Bourbon BELIEF was first conceived, it was not just intended to be another bourbon on the market. It was designed to be something much more—a symbol of heritage, a testament to belief, and a legacy that would endure for generations. With only 200 bottles produced, each one represents a piece of history, a tangible reminder of the values that underpin Di Tran Enterprises. These bottles are not just collectibles; they are a manifestation of a dream, a story, and a commitment to something greater than just the product itself.

Di Tran Bourbon BELIEF is, at its core, about the power of belief—the belief that we can create something extraordinary when we stay true to our values, our heritage, and our community. It is a bourbon that transcends the ordinary, embodying the spirit of excellence, authenticity, and community that defines Di Tran Enterprises. As the company continues to grow, this bourbon remains a symbol of its unwavering commitment to these principles, serving as a beacon for what can be achieved when we believe in something deeply and work tirelessly to bring it to life.

Kentucky Bourbon: The Pride of the Bluegrass State
Di Tran Bourbon BELIEF: Bridging American Bourbon to the World

The Pride of Kentucky: A Land of Opportunity

Kentucky is a place like no other—a land of rolling hills, fertile soil, and rich history. It is a state that has been blessed with natural resources that have made it the perfect home for bourbon production. The limestone-rich water, the fertile soil that nurtures the bluegrass, and the unique climate that supports both the aging of bourbon and the raising of world-class horses all come together to create a place that is as unique as it is beautiful. Kentucky is not just a state; it is a legacy in itself, a land that has been entrusted to us to care for and to pass on to future generations.

For Di Tran, Kentucky is more than just a place where he lives and works; it is a land that welcomed him as an immigrant and offered him the opportunity to build a life, a business, and a legacy. It is a place that represents the American dream—the idea that anyone, regardless of where they come from, can achieve great things if they work hard, stay true to their values, and believe in themselves. Di Tran Bourbon BELIEF is a celebration of this dream, a tribute to the state that has given so much to so many.

Immigrant Pride: A Shared Heritage

The story of Di Tran Bourbon BELIEF is also the story of America—a nation built by immigrants, each

Kentucky Bourbon: The Pride of the Bluegrass State
Di Tran Bourbon BELIEF: Bridging American Bourbon to the World

bringing their own unique cultures, traditions, and dreams to create something greater than the sum of its parts. Di Tran's journey from Vietnam to Kentucky is one of countless similar stories that have shaped the fabric of this country. It is a story of perseverance, hope, and the belief that a better life is possible through hard work and dedication.

In this sense, Di Tran Bourbon BELIEF is not just a product of Kentucky; it is a product of the immigrant experience. It embodies the spirit of those who have come to this country in search of a better life, who have worked tirelessly to build something of value, and who have contributed to the rich tapestry that makes America what it is today. This bourbon is a tribute to all immigrants, past and present, who have made sacrifices, overcome challenges, and paved the way for future generations. It is a reminder that, at its core, America is a nation of immigrants, each bringing their own unique contributions to the collective whole.

A Testament to the God-Given Land of Kentucky

Kentucky is a land blessed by God—a place where the natural beauty of the landscape is matched by the richness of its resources. The limestone that filters the water, the bluegrass that covers the rolling hills, the horses that grace the fields, and the bourbon that ages

Kentucky Bourbon: The Pride of the Bluegrass State
Di Tran Bourbon BELIEF: Bridging American Bourbon to the World

in barrels—each of these is a gift, a reminder of the divine hand that has shaped this land. Di Tran Bourbon BELIEF is a celebration of this God-given bounty, a recognition of the blessings that have made Kentucky the perfect place for bourbon production.

The limestone-rich water of Kentucky is often cited as one of the key factors that make its bourbon so special. This water, filtered through ancient limestone deposits, is free of iron and rich in calcium, making it ideal for distilling bourbon. It is this water that gives Kentucky bourbon its unique character, its smoothness, and its rich flavor. Di Tran Bourbon BELIEF is a testament to the importance of this natural resource, a reminder that the land itself is an essential part of the bourbon-making process.

The bluegrass that covers the hills of Kentucky is another gift from God, providing the perfect environment for raising world-class horses and for growing the grains that are essential to bourbon production. The climate of Kentucky, with its hot summers and cold winters, is ideal for aging bourbon, allowing the spirit to expand and contract within the barrels, drawing out the rich flavors of the charred oak. Di Tran Bourbon BELIEF is a tribute to this climate, a recognition of the role that the seasons play in shaping the character of the bourbon.

Kentucky Bourbon: The Pride of the Bluegrass State
Di Tran Bourbon BELIEF: Bridging American Bourbon to the World

The Culture of Love and Care

Kentucky is not just known for its natural beauty and resources; it is also known for its culture of love, care, and community. It is a place where people look out for one another, where neighbors are more than just people who live next door—they are friends, family, and an essential part of the social fabric. This culture of love and care is something that Di Tran has experienced firsthand, both as an immigrant and as a member of the Kentucky community.

When Di Tran and his family first arrived in Kentucky, they were welcomed with open arms by organizations like the Kentucky Refugee Ministries and Catholic Charities. These organizations, along with countless individuals in the community, provided the support and resources that Di Tran and his family needed to build a new life in America. This spirit of generosity and care is something that Di Tran has never forgotten, and it is something that he strives to embody in everything he does.

Di Tran Bourbon BELIEF is a reflection of this culture of love and care. It is a bourbon that is meant to be shared, to bring people together, and to foster a sense of community. The proceeds from each bottle sold go towards charitable causes, reinforcing the belief that

Kentucky Bourbon: The Pride of the Bluegrass State
Di Tran Bourbon BELIEF: Bridging American Bourbon to the World

business should be a force for good. This commitment to giving back is a core part of the legacy that Di Tran Bourbon BELIEF aims to create—a legacy that is rooted in the values of love, care, and community.

Honoring Those Who Came Before Us

In creating Di Tran Bourbon BELIEF, there is a deep sense of gratitude for those who came before us—those who paved the way, who made sacrifices, and who laid the foundations upon which we now build. This bourbon is a tribute to the generations of Kentuckians who have contributed to the state's rich heritage, from the pioneers who first settled the land to the master distillers who perfected the art of bourbon making. It is a recognition of the importance of honoring the past, even as we look towards the future.

Di Tran Bourbon BELIEF is also a tribute to the immigrants who have come to America in search of a better life, who have brought their own unique cultures, traditions, and perspectives to this great nation. It is a reminder that we are all part of a larger story, one that spans generations and that connects us to both our ancestors and to future generations. By honoring those who came before us, we are also laying the groundwork for those who will come after us,

Kentucky Bourbon: The Pride of the Bluegrass State
Di Tran Bourbon BELIEF: Bridging American Bourbon to the World

ensuring that the legacy of Di Tran Bourbon BELIEF will continue to inspire and uplift for years to come.

A Vision for the Future: Going National and Global

While Di Tran Bourbon BELIEF is deeply rooted in Kentucky, its vision extends far beyond the borders of the state. Once firmly established in Kentucky, the goal is to take this bourbon national and global, sharing the spirit of Kentucky with the world. This vision is not just about expanding the reach of the brand; it is about sharing the values that Di Tran Bourbon BELIEF represents—values of excellence, authenticity, community, and giving back.

Vietnam and other parts of Asia represent significant opportunities for expansion, particularly given Di Tran's deep connections to the region. By introducing Di Tran Bourbon BELIEF to these markets, the goal is to create a bridge between cultures, one that celebrates both the heritage of Kentucky and the traditions of Asia. This expansion is not just about selling bourbon; it is about creating connections, fostering understanding, and building a global community that is united by shared values and a love of fine spirits.

As Di Tran Bourbon BELIEF expands its reach, it will continue to stay true to its roots, ensuring that the values of quality, authenticity, and community remain

Kentucky Bourbon: The Pride of the Bluegrass State
Di Tran Bourbon BELIEF: Bridging American Bourbon to the World

at the heart of everything it does. This commitment to staying true to its values, even as it grows, is what will ensure that the legacy of Di Tran Bourbon BELIEF endures for generations to come.

The Collective Elevation of Humanity and Spirit

At the heart of Di Tran Bourbon BELIEF is a profound belief in the collective elevation of humanity and spirit. This bourbon is not just about the drink itself; it is about what the drink represents—a belief that we can come together, support one another, and elevate each other to new heights. It is about recognizing that we are all connected, that our actions have an impact on others, and that by working together, we can create a better world.

This belief is reflected in every aspect of Di Tran Bourbon BELIEF, from the quality of the bourbon to the charitable causes that it supports. It is a belief that business should be a force for good, that success is not just measured in profits, but in the positive impact that we have on the world around us. By creating a bourbon that is rooted in these values, Di Tran is contributing to the collective elevation of humanity and spirit, helping to build a legacy that will inspire and uplift for generations to come.

A Legacy of Love and Gratitude

Kentucky Bourbon: The Pride of the Bluegrass State
Di Tran Bourbon BELIEF: Bridging American Bourbon to the World

As Di Tran Bourbon BELIEF continues to grow and evolve, it will remain true to the values that have guided it from the beginning—values of love, gratitude, and community. This bourbon is a testament to the power of belief, a reminder that when we stay true to our values and work together, we can achieve great things. It is a legacy that is built on love—love for Kentucky, love for the immigrant experience, and love for the community that has supported and nurtured Di Tran along the way.

This legacy is also one of gratitude—gratitude for the opportunities that Kentucky has provided, for the support of the community, and for the chance to create something that will have a lasting impact. Di Tran Bourbon BELIEF is a way to give back, to honor those who have come before us, and to contribute to the ongoing story of Kentucky and the immigrant experience. It is a legacy that will continue to grow, to inspire, and to uplift for generations to come.

Conclusion: Beyond the Bottle

Di Tran Bourbon BELIEF is more than just a bourbon; it is a legacy in the making. It is a symbol of the power of belief, of the importance of staying true to our values, and of the potential for business to be a force for good. With only 200 bottles produced, each one

Kentucky Bourbon: The Pride of the Bluegrass State
Di Tran Bourbon BELIEF: Bridging American Bourbon to the World

represents a piece of history, a tangible reminder of the values that underpin Di Tran Enterprises. But beyond the bottle, Di Tran Bourbon BELIEF is about something much larger—it is about the collective elevation of humanity and spirit, about creating a legacy of love, gratitude, and community that will endure for generations to come.

As Di Tran Bourbon BELIEF continues to grow, expanding its reach both nationally and globally, it will remain rooted in the values that have guided it from the beginning. It will continue to celebrate the heritage of Kentucky, the immigrant experience, and the God-given beauty of the land. And it will continue to give back, supporting charitable causes and contributing to the collective elevation of humanity and spirit. This is the legacy of Di Tran Bourbon BELIEF—a legacy that goes beyond the bottle, beyond the bourbon, and into the very heart of what it means to believe.

Kentucky Bourbon: The Pride of the Bluegrass State
Di Tran Bourbon BELIEF: Bridging American Bourbon to the World

Chapter 9: The Global Spirit of Kentucky

Kentucky Bourbon: A Global Ambassador

Kentucky bourbon is more than just a local treasure; it is a symbol of American craftsmanship, a spirit that represents the rich cultural heritage of the United States. Over the years, Kentucky bourbon has earned its place on the global stage, standing shoulder to shoulder with some of the world's most iconic spirits, such as French Cognac and Irish whiskey. Among the many bourbons that Kentucky produces, Di Tran Bourbon BELIEF stands out as a unique and powerful representation of what this state has to offer—a bourbon that not only embodies the essence of Kentucky but also has the potential to become a global ambassador for American excellence.

As the world continues to embrace premium spirits, the demand for high-quality, authentic bourbon is growing. Di Tran Bourbon BELIEF, with its deep roots in Kentucky's rich bourbon-making tradition and its commitment to quality, is perfectly positioned to meet this demand. However, to truly take Di Tran Bourbon BELIEF global, there is a need for strategic investment, partnerships, and support from those who believe in the potential of this exceptional bourbon.

Kentucky Bourbon: The Pride of the Bluegrass State
Di Tran Bourbon BELIEF: Bridging American Bourbon to the World

This chapter explores the opportunities for investors, funders, bankers, and global businesses to invest in Di Tran Bourbon BELIEF and help share the spirit of Kentucky with the world.

Bourbon vs. The World: A Unique Offering

In the world of premium spirits, each category has its own distinct characteristics that set it apart. Cognac, for instance, is celebrated for its refined elegance and deep connection to French culture. It is a spirit that is often associated with sophistication, luxury, and a certain old-world charm. Irish whiskey, on the other hand, is known for its smoothness and rich heritage, often enjoyed in a more casual setting but no less revered for its quality and craftsmanship.

Kentucky bourbon, however, offers something entirely different—a unique blend of sweetness, spice, and strength that is the result of centuries of tradition and the unique conditions found only in Kentucky. The use of corn as the primary grain in bourbon gives it a natural sweetness that is balanced by the bold flavors imparted by the charred oak barrels in which it is aged. The climate of Kentucky, with its hot summers and cold winters, further enhances the aging process, creating a spirit that is both complex and approachable.

Kentucky Bourbon: The Pride of the Bluegrass State
Di Tran Bourbon BELIEF: Bridging American Bourbon to the World

Di Tran Bourbon BELIEF takes these qualities to the next level. Aged for eight years and bottled straight from the barrel, this bourbon offers a full-bodied, rich flavor that is both smooth and powerful. It is a bourbon that commands attention, a spirit that can stand proudly alongside the finest Cognacs and Irish whiskeys of the world. But more than just a drink, Di Tran Bourbon BELIEF is a representation of the American spirit—bold, innovative, and deeply rooted in tradition.

The Role of Investment in Taking Di Tran Bourbon Global

To fully realize the potential of Di Tran Bourbon BELIEF on the global stage, strategic investment is crucial. The global spirits market is highly competitive, with established brands and emerging players all vying for attention. However, the unique qualities of Di Tran Bourbon BELIEF—its exceptional flavor profile, its rich heritage, and its commitment to authenticity—give it a distinct advantage. With the right investment, this bourbon can become a leading global brand, representing the best of what Kentucky and America have to offer.

Investors have a unique opportunity to be part of this journey, to support the expansion of Di Tran Bourbon BELIEF into new markets and to help build a brand

Kentucky Bourbon: The Pride of the Bluegrass State
Di Tran Bourbon BELIEF: Bridging American Bourbon to the World

that stands for quality, tradition, and innovation. This investment goes beyond just financial support; it is an investment in a vision, in a belief that Di Tran Bourbon BELIEF can become a global ambassador for Kentucky bourbon. It is an investment in the future of American craftsmanship and in the potential for this bourbon to create connections and foster unity around the world.

Opportunities for Funders and Bankers

Funders and bankers also play a critical role in the global expansion of Di Tran Bourbon BELIEF. The production, distribution, and marketing of a premium spirit on a global scale require significant resources, and the support of financial institutions is essential to making this vision a reality. By providing the necessary funding, these institutions can help ensure that Di Tran Bourbon BELIEF has the resources it needs to compete in the global marketplace.

Beyond just providing capital, funders and bankers can also offer strategic advice and support, helping to navigate the complexities of international markets and ensuring that Di Tran Bourbon BELIEF is positioned for success. This partnership is not just about funding a product; it is about supporting a brand that has the potential to make a significant impact on the global

Kentucky Bourbon: The Pride of the Bluegrass State
Di Tran Bourbon BELIEF: Bridging American Bourbon to the World

spirits market. It is about being part of a journey to take a uniquely American product and share it with the world.

Global Business Partnerships: Expanding the Reach of Di Tran Bourbon BELIEF

Global business partnerships are another key component of taking Di Tran Bourbon BELIEF to the next level. By partnering with distributors, retailers, and other businesses around the world, Di Tran Bourbon BELIEF can expand its reach and introduce this exceptional bourbon to new audiences. These partnerships are essential for building brand awareness, establishing a presence in new markets, and ensuring that Di Tran Bourbon BELIEF is available to consumers around the globe.

For global businesses, partnering with Di Tran Bourbon BELIEF offers a unique opportunity to be part of a brand that is not just about selling a product but about promoting a philosophy of quality, authenticity, and unity. This bourbon is more than just a drink; it is a symbol of what can be achieved when we believe in something deeply and work together to bring that vision to life. By partnering with Di Tran Bourbon BELIEF, global businesses can be part of a movement to share the spirit of Kentucky with the

Kentucky Bourbon: The Pride of the Bluegrass State
Di Tran Bourbon BELIEF: Bridging American Bourbon to the World

world and to create connections that transcend borders and cultures.

The Unity of Bonding Through Bourbon

At its core, Di Tran Bourbon BELIEF is about more than just bourbon; it is about the connections that are formed when people come together to share a drink. Bourbon has a unique ability to bring people together, to foster conversation, and to create bonds that go beyond the surface. This is particularly true of Di Tran Bourbon BELIEF, which is crafted with the intention of creating moments of connection, of bringing people together in a spirit of unity and celebration.

As Di Tran Bourbon BELIEF expands its reach globally, it has the potential to become a symbol of unity, a drink that transcends cultural and geographic boundaries and brings people together in a shared experience. Whether it's enjoyed in a quiet moment of reflection or shared among friends at a celebration, Di Tran Bourbon BELIEF is a reminder of the power of connection, of the belief that we are better when we are united. This is the essence of Di Tran Bourbon BELIEF—a spirit that is not just about what's in the bottle but about the experiences, the connections, and the bonds that it helps to create.

Kentucky's Creation on the Global Stage

Kentucky Bourbon: The Pride of the Bluegrass State
Di Tran Bourbon BELIEF: Bridging American Bourbon to the World

Kentucky bourbon has long been a symbol of American craftsmanship, a product that is deeply connected to the land, the people, and the culture of Kentucky. As Di Tran Bourbon BELIEF takes its place on the global stage, it carries with it the legacy of Kentucky, a legacy that is built on a foundation of quality, tradition, and a deep respect for the craft of bourbon making.

This bourbon is a tribute to the belief that Kentucky bourbon is not just a drink but a global ambassador for American excellence. It is a product that represents the best of what America has to offer—a commitment to quality, a dedication to craftsmanship, and a belief in the power of community. As Di Tran Bourbon BELIEF expands its reach, it will continue to uphold these values, sharing the spirit of Kentucky with the world and promoting the legacy of American bourbon on a global scale.

Building a Legacy: The Future of Di Tran Bourbon BELIEF

The future of Di Tran Bourbon BELIEF is bright, but it will require the support and investment of those who believe in its potential to truly achieve its global ambitions. By investing in Di Tran Bourbon BELIEF, funders, bankers, and global businesses have the

Kentucky Bourbon: The Pride of the Bluegrass State
Di Tran Bourbon BELIEF: Bridging American Bourbon to the World

opportunity to be part of something truly special—a brand that is not just about selling bourbon but about creating a legacy, a movement, and a global community that is united by a shared love of quality, tradition, and connection.

This legacy is not just about the success of Di Tran Bourbon BELIEF as a product; it is about the impact that it can have on the world. By bringing people together, fostering connections, and promoting a philosophy of unity and excellence, Di Tran Bourbon BELIEF has the potential to make a lasting impact on the global spirits market and beyond. It is a legacy that will continue to grow, to inspire, and to connect people around the world for generations to come.

Conclusion: A Global Ambassador of American Craftsmanship

Di Tran Bourbon BELIEF is more than just a bourbon; it is a global ambassador of American craftsmanship, a product that represents the best of what Kentucky and America have to offer. As this bourbon continues to expand its reach, it will bring with it the values of quality, tradition, and unity that have defined its creation. But to achieve its full potential, Di Tran Bourbon BELIEF will require the support of investors,

Kentucky Bourbon: The Pride of the Bluegrass State
Di Tran Bourbon BELIEF: Bridging American Bourbon to the World

funders, bankers, and global businesses who believe in its vision and who are willing to invest in its future.

By partnering with Di Tran Bourbon BELIEF, these stakeholders have the opportunity to be part of a brand that is not just about selling a product but about creating a movement, a legacy, and a global community that is united by a shared love of bourbon and the connections that it helps to create. This is the promise of Di Tran Bourbon BELIEF—a spirit that transcends the bottle, that goes beyond the drink, and that has the potential to bring people together in a spirit of unity and celebration. As it takes its place on the global stage, Di Tran Bourbon BELIEF will continue to represent the best of Kentucky, the best of America, and the best of what it means to believe.

Chapter 10: The Future of Bourbon – Continuing the Tradition

A Legacy Worth Preserving

Kentucky bourbon has long been a symbol of American craftsmanship, a testament to the values of quality, tradition, and community that have defined the region for centuries. From the rolling hills of bluegrass to the limestone-filtered waters, Kentucky is a land that has been uniquely blessed, and it is this blessing that has given birth to one of the world's most beloved spirits. But the story of Kentucky bourbon is not just one of the past; it is a story that continues to unfold, with each new generation adding its own chapter to this rich legacy.

The release of Di Tran Bourbon BELIEF marks the beginning of a new chapter in this ongoing story. As bourbon continues to grow in popularity worldwide, the future holds endless possibilities for those who are willing to embrace both tradition and innovation. Di Tran Enterprises, with its deep respect for the heritage of Kentucky bourbon and its unique perspective as a company that is "Vietnamese Born and American Made," is poised to carry this tradition forward in ways

Kentucky Bourbon: The Pride of the Bluegrass State
Di Tran Bourbon BELIEF: Bridging American Bourbon to the World

that honor the past while also looking boldly toward the future.

The Growing Popularity of Bourbon Worldwide

Bourbon has seen a remarkable rise in popularity over the past few decades, not just in the United States, but across the globe. From the bustling streets of Tokyo to the refined lounges of London, bourbon has become a symbol of American culture and craftsmanship, celebrated for its rich flavors, its versatility, and its deep connection to the land from which it comes. This growing demand for bourbon presents a unique opportunity for brands like Di Tran Bourbon BELIEF to expand their reach and share the spirit of Kentucky with the world.

The global appeal of bourbon lies in its ability to transcend cultural boundaries. Whether enjoyed neat, on the rocks, or as the base of a cocktail, bourbon offers something for everyone. Its complex flavor profile, which combines sweetness, spice, and strength, makes it a versatile spirit that can be enjoyed in a variety of settings and by people from all walks of life. This versatility is one of the key reasons why bourbon has become so popular worldwide, and it is also what makes it such an exciting prospect for future growth.

Kentucky Bourbon: The Pride of the Bluegrass State
Di Tran Bourbon BELIEF: Bridging American Bourbon to the World

Di Tran Bourbon BELIEF, with its commitment to quality and tradition, is uniquely positioned to take advantage of this growing global interest in bourbon. By staying true to the values that have made Kentucky bourbon what it is today, while also embracing the opportunities that come with going global, Di Tran Enterprises can help ensure that bourbon continues to thrive for generations to come.

Innovation Meets Tradition: The Di Tran Approach

One of the defining characteristics of Di Tran Bourbon BELIEF is its ability to blend innovation with tradition. This is not just a bourbon that is content to rest on its laurels; it is a bourbon that is constantly looking for ways to push the boundaries of what is possible, while still remaining true to the heritage that has made Kentucky bourbon so special.

This commitment to innovation is evident in every aspect of Di Tran Bourbon BELIEF, from the way it is produced to the way it is marketed. For instance, the decision to bottle the bourbon straight from the barrel, without dilution, is a nod to the traditional methods of bourbon making, while also offering something unique to today's discerning consumers. This approach allows the true character of the bourbon to shine through,

Kentucky Bourbon: The Pride of the Bluegrass State
Di Tran Bourbon BELIEF: Bridging American Bourbon to the World

giving drinkers an experience that is both authentic and unparalleled.

At the same time, Di Tran Enterprises is also committed to exploring new ways to bring bourbon to the world. This includes not only expanding into new markets but also finding innovative ways to connect with consumers and share the story of Di Tran Bourbon BELIEF. Whether through collaborations with other brands, unique marketing campaigns, or partnerships with global distributors, Di Tran Enterprises is always looking for ways to grow the brand and ensure that the legacy of Kentucky bourbon continues to thrive.

The Influence of Vietnamese Culture: A Unique Perspective

One of the most exciting aspects of Di Tran Bourbon BELIEF is the unique perspective that it brings to the world of bourbon. As a company that is "Vietnamese Born and American Made," Di Tran Enterprises is able to draw on the rich cultural traditions of both Vietnam and the United States, blending these influences in ways that create something truly special.

Vietnamese culture, with its deep respect for tradition, its emphasis on community, and its appreciation for the finer things in life, aligns closely with the values that

Kentucky Bourbon: The Pride of the Bluegrass State
Di Tran Bourbon BELIEF: Bridging American Bourbon to the World

have long been associated with Kentucky bourbon. At the same time, the entrepreneurial spirit and innovative mindset that characterize the Vietnamese-American experience add a fresh and dynamic element to the brand, allowing Di Tran Bourbon BELIEF to stand out in a crowded market.

This blending of cultures is not just about creating a unique product; it is also about creating a brand that resonates with a diverse and global audience. By drawing on the strengths of both Vietnamese and American traditions, Di Tran Enterprises is able to craft a bourbon that is both deeply rooted in tradition and forward-looking, a product that appeals to both long-time bourbon enthusiasts and those who are just discovering the spirit for the first time.

Building a Global Brand: The Next Steps

As Di Tran Bourbon BELIEF continues to grow, the next logical step is to expand its reach beyond the borders of the United States and into the global market. This is not just about selling more bottles of bourbon; it is about sharing the story of Di Tran Bourbon BELIEF with the world, about bringing people together through the shared experience of enjoying a fine spirit, and about continuing the legacy of Kentucky bourbon on a global scale.

Kentucky Bourbon: The Pride of the Bluegrass State
Di Tran Bourbon BELIEF: Bridging American Bourbon to the World

To achieve this, Di Tran Enterprises is committed to building strong partnerships with distributors, retailers, and other stakeholders around the world. These partnerships are essential for ensuring that Di Tran Bourbon BELIEF is available to consumers in key markets, from Asia to Europe to South America. By working with partners who share the company's commitment to quality and authenticity, Di Tran Enterprises can help ensure that the brand continues to grow in a way that is true to its values.

At the same time, Di Tran Enterprises is also focused on creating a strong brand identity that resonates with consumers around the world. This includes not only the product itself but also the story behind it—the story of a bourbon that is born in Kentucky, shaped by Vietnamese culture, and made with a deep respect for tradition. By telling this story in a way that is both compelling and authentic, Di Tran Enterprises can help ensure that Di Tran Bourbon BELIEF becomes a global brand that is recognized and respected by consumers everywhere.

The Importance of Community and Giving Back

As Di Tran Bourbon BELIEF continues to grow, one thing will always remain at the heart of the brand: a commitment to community and giving back. This is a

Kentucky Bourbon: The Pride of the Bluegrass State
Di Tran Bourbon BELIEF: Bridging American Bourbon to the World

core value that has been part of Di Tran Enterprises from the very beginning, and it is something that will continue to guide the company as it moves forward.

For Di Tran, bourbon is not just about making a great product; it is also about making a positive impact on the world. This is why a portion of the proceeds from each bottle of Di Tran Bourbon BELIEF is donated to charitable causes, supporting initiatives that help to build stronger communities and improve the lives of those in need. This commitment to giving back is not just a marketing strategy; it is a fundamental part of the company's mission and a reflection of the values that have guided Di Tran throughout his life.

As Di Tran Bourbon BELIEF expands into new markets, this commitment to community and giving back will continue to play a central role in the brand's identity. Whether through partnerships with local organizations, support for global initiatives, or contributions to causes that resonate with consumers, Di Tran Enterprises is dedicated to using its success to make a positive difference in the world.

A Future Rooted in Tradition

As the future of bourbon continues to unfold, one thing is clear: the tradition of Kentucky bourbon is alive and well, and it is being carried forward by brands like Di

Kentucky Bourbon: The Pride of the Bluegrass State
Di Tran Bourbon BELIEF: Bridging American Bourbon to the World

Tran Bourbon BELIEF. This is a bourbon that is deeply rooted in the values that have made Kentucky bourbon what it is today—quality, tradition, and community—while also embracing the possibilities of the future.

For Di Tran, the future of bourbon is not just about continuing the legacy of the past; it is also about creating new traditions, new stories, and new connections that will carry the spirit of Kentucky bourbon forward for generations to come. This is a future that is filled with possibilities, and it is one that Di Tran Enterprises is committed to exploring with the same passion, dedication, and belief that has guided the company from the very beginning.

As Di Tran Bourbon BELIEF continues to grow, it will remain true to the values that have defined it from the start. It will continue to be a bourbon that is made with love, with respect for the land and the people who make it possible, and with a commitment to creating something truly special. And as it expands its reach around the world, it will carry with it the spirit of Kentucky, the traditions of Vietnamese culture, and the belief that, when we come together to celebrate the good things in life, we can create a legacy that will endure for generations.

Kentucky Bourbon: The Pride of the Bluegrass State
Di Tran Bourbon BELIEF: Bridging American Bourbon to the World

Vietnamese Born, American Made: A Global Legacy

The story of Di Tran Bourbon BELIEF is, in many ways, the story of the American dream—a story of a young man who came to the United States from Vietnam in search of a better life, and who found that life in the rolling hills of Kentucky. It is a story of hard work, of perseverance, and of a deep belief in the power of tradition and innovation. But it is also a story that goes beyond the borders of Kentucky and the United States, a story that has the potential to resonate with people around the world.

As Di Tran Bourbon BELIEF continues to grow, it will carry with it the legacy of both Vietnam and America, blending these two rich traditions in a way that creates something truly unique. This is a bourbon that is born in the heart of Kentucky, but that is shaped by the experiences, the values, and the culture of Vietnam. It is a bourbon that is American-made, but that carries with it the spirit of a global citizen—someone who understands the importance of honoring the past while also embracing the future.

The future of Di Tran Bourbon BELIEF is one that is filled with promise, not just for the brand itself, but for the global community that it will help to create. By

Kentucky Bourbon: The Pride of the Bluegrass State
Di Tran Bourbon BELIEF: Bridging American Bourbon to the World

sharing the story of this bourbon with the world, Di Tran Enterprises is helping to build bridges between cultures, to create connections that transcend borders, and to carry forward the tradition of Kentucky bourbon in a way that honors the past while also looking toward the future.

Conclusion: A Tradition Worth Carrying Forward

The release of Di Tran Bourbon BELIEF is just the beginning of a journey that will continue to unfold in the years to come. As bourbon continues to grow in popularity worldwide, the future holds endless possibilities for those who are willing to embrace both tradition and innovation. Di Tran Enterprises, with its unique perspective as a company that is "Vietnamese Born and American Made," is poised to carry the tradition of Kentucky bourbon forward in ways that honor the past while also looking boldly toward the future.

This is a tradition worth carrying forward—not just for the sake of the bourbon itself, but for the sake of the values that it represents. It is a tradition of quality, of community, of respect for the land and the people who make it possible. It is a tradition that is rooted in the rolling hills of Kentucky, but that has the potential to reach every corner of the globe. And it is a tradition

Kentucky Bourbon: The Pride of the Bluegrass State
Di Tran Bourbon BELIEF: Bridging American Bourbon to the World

that, with the support of those who believe in it, will continue to thrive for generations to come.

Kentucky Bourbon: The Pride of the Bluegrass State
Di Tran Bourbon BELIEF: Bridging American Bourbon to the World

Conclusion: The Spirit of Di Tran Bourbon BELIEF

In every sip of Di Tran Bourbon BELIEF, there is a story—a story of tradition, heritage, and a belief in something greater than ourselves. This bourbon, born in the rolling hills of Kentucky and nurtured by the rich cultural traditions of Vietnam, is more than just a drink. It is a symbol of connection, unity, and the power of belief to transcend borders, cultures, and generations.

For Di Tran, bourbon has always been about more than just the liquid in the glass. It's about the moments that are shared, the bonds that are formed, and the connections that are deepened when people come together to enjoy a fine spirit. Sipping bourbon is not just an act of indulgence; it is an experience that invites us to be present, to connect with those around us, and to engage in a dialogue with the universe, with God, and with the higher beings that guide our lives.

Di Tran Bourbon BELIEF is crafted with this philosophy at its core. It is a bourbon that is meant to be savored, to be enjoyed in the company of those who resonate with us on the same frequency, who share our values, and who enrich our lives with their presence. Whether you are gathered with family, friends,

Kentucky Bourbon: The Pride of the Bluegrass State
Di Tran Bourbon BELIEF: Bridging American Bourbon to the World

business partners, or close ones, Di Tran Bourbon BELIEF serves as a catalyst for meaningful conversations, bonding in spirit, and fostering a sense of love and care that transcends the ordinary.

This bourbon is not just about Kentucky, though it is deeply rooted in the traditions of this proud state. It is also about the broader world, about taking the spirit of Kentucky bourbon and sharing it with people around the globe. Di Tran Bourbon BELIEF is poised to grow, first in Louisville, then throughout the USA, and eventually across the world, particularly in Vietnam and Asia, where it can stand proudly alongside other iconic drinks.

As Di Tran Bourbon BELIEF expands its reach, it will carry with it the values that have defined it from the beginning: a commitment to quality, a respect for tradition, and a belief in the power of connection. This bourbon is not just a product; it is a testament to what can be achieved when we believe in something deeply and work together to bring that belief to life.

For those seeking an investment opportunity that aligns with these values—something truly special—Di Tran Enterprises (Di Tran LLC) offers a partnership like no other. Di Tran Bourbon represents the best of Kentucky, delivering quality in vision, mission, love,

Kentucky Bourbon: The Pride of the Bluegrass State
Di Tran Bourbon BELIEF: Bridging American Bourbon to the World

care, and people. Investing in Di Tran Enterprises means investing in a company that is committed to excellence, that values its community, and that is dedicated to creating a legacy that will endure for generations.

In the end, Di Tran Bourbon BELIEF is about more than just bourbon. It is about the spirit of unity, love, and care that binds us all together. It is about creating a legacy rooted in the traditions of Kentucky, but one that reaches out to embrace the world. It is about the belief that when we come together to celebrate the good things in life, we can create something truly special—a bond that transcends time, place, and culture.

So here's to Di Tran Bourbon BELIEF, to the spirit of Kentucky, to the traditions of Vietnam, and to the belief that we are all part of something greater. Here's to the moments we share, the connections we make, and the legacy we leave behind. Here's to the future of bourbon, and to the belief that, together, we can create a world where love, unity, and care are at the heart of everything we do. And for those who wish to be part of something extraordinary, Di Tran Enterprises is the best partner for your journey.

Kentucky Bourbon: The Pride of the Bluegrass State
Di Tran Bourbon BELIEF: Bridging American Bourbon to the World

God is Beautiful, So is His Creation

God is beautiful, and so the universe He made,
In every star, in every blade,
With Di Tran Bourbon BELIEF in hand,
We taste the love across this land.

A sip of bourbon, rich and pure,
Brings the universe's energy, strong and sure,
It bridges hearts, it bonds us tight,
In love and care, we find our light.

Each glass raised is more than cheer,
It's a moment shared, with those held dear,
Each conversation, each story told,
Is a thread in the fabric of love we hold.

For each of us has loved ones near,
In every smile, in every tear,
As Di Tran with his three sons grows,
In family, in love, the spirit flows.

We drink to life, to bonds unbroken,
To words of love, so softly spoken,
In every sip, in every glance,
We find God's beauty, His eternal dance.

Kentucky Bourbon: The Pride of the Bluegrass State
Di Tran Bourbon BELIEF: Bridging American Bourbon to the World

So let us care, and let us share,
With every sip, a love laid bare,
For in this bourbon, rich and deep,
We find a promise we all shall keep.

To love, to bond, to hold so tight,
To bring each other into the light,
God is beautiful, and so are we,
Bound by love, in unity.

Kentucky Bourbon: The Pride of the Bluegrass State
Di Tran Bourbon BELIEF: Bridging American Bourbon to the World

THE END

THANK YOU

www.ingramcontent.com/pod-product-compliance
Lightning Source LLC
Chambersburg PA
CBHW050315230526
45471CB00005B/2189